Tap into Joy

A Guide to Emotional Freedom Techniques for Kids and Their Parents

Susan Jeffrey Busen
Foreword by Carol Tuttle

Digital Legend Press

Tap into Joy

A Guide to Emotional Freedom Techniques for Kids and Their Parents

Books may be ordered by sending e-mail to digitallegender@gmail.com

Digital Legend Press
New York
(585)624-5641

www.digitallegendpress.com

The information, ideas, and suggestions in this book are not intended as a substitute for professional advice. Before following any suggestions contained in this book, you should consult your personal physician or mental health professional. Neither the author nor the publisher shall be liable or responsible for any loss or damage allegedly arising as a consequence of your use or application of any information or suggestions in this book. The information and suggestions in this book are not intended to diagnose, treat, cure or prevent any condition.

ISBN-13: 978-1-974537-70-1

ISBN-10: 1-934537-70-5

Printed in the United States of America

For their love and support, this work is dedicated to my family, and to the memory of my dad and my brother.

Whether you think you can or you think you can't;
either way you are right,

Henry Ford

CONTENTS

FOREWORD

Energy Therapy is a valuable tool for our time. We no longer have to carry the issues of our childhood into our adult years only to be confronted with them later. Sue Busen's book, *Tap into Joy: A Guide to Emotional Freedom Techniques for Kids and Their Parents*, is an important tool to ensure that as adults and parents we aid our children in preventing this scenario. As we use this book with our children, we empower them to address and take care of their emotional experience. We validate their experience, and teach them to release the emotional energy so they do not have to carry this energy only to clear it years later.

Emotional Freedom Techniques (EFT) is one of the simplest and most effective energy therapy tools to use. I highly encourage anyone that is involved with children, such as parents, grandparents, childcare providers, teachers, and coaches, to utilize the methods and information shared in this book.

Energy therapy and EFT are a gift to our planet. Our children are ready to learn and will welcome the support. Children are more emotionally advanced than we were as children. If there is any hesitation to teach this to the children in your life, that would be your fear, not theirs. If that is the case, use this book for yourself before you use it with them. Better yet, use it along with them. You will create amazing, enlightening experiences together.

God bless you as you proceed.

Carol Tuttle

Master Energy Therapist

Author of *Remembering Wholeness*

www.caroltuttle.com

PREFACE

Special Message to Children and Teens

This book is going to teach you a very awesome way to make you feel better. It uses something called Emotional Freedom Techniques. Emotional Freedom Techniques is also called EFT or tapping. You can use tapping anytime something bothers you. You can use it all of your life—even when you are a grown-up.

You might be wondering how tapping works. Tapping is easy. You use your fingers to tap on very special points on your hands, face, and body. You say special words at the same time you are tapping. All you have to do is think about the problem and decide which part of the book best describes how you feel. Your parents can help you decide.

Tapping helps to take away bad feelings. Bad feelings have bad energy. We want to get the bad energy out of your body. If you feel sad, mad, frustrated, or afraid, then the bad energy of those feelings is not getting out of your body. When you tap, you are helping your body get rid of the bad energy. The bad energy then gets replaced with good energy. Good energy feelings make you feel happy, calm, peaceful, brave, and free to have lots of joy in your life.

You and your parents are about to go on an awesome journey. Join me and tap into joy!

Message to EFT Practitioners and Energy Therapists

This guide is designed to be an invaluable tool for you and your clients. I encourage you to provide them with a copy of this book so that they can resolve minor issues between visits. This will help them to make permanent lasting shifts away from negative energy blocks and will make your sessions with them more effective.

As with most energy therapies, practitioners put their own unique twist on the techniques. There may be a few steps that I have included that you are not currently using or perhaps you are using other procedures that I am not. I generally use the points presented here in addition to the Nine Gamut Point procedure in my private sessions. I have attempted to simplify and standardize the process for this book. I honor the work that you are doing, and I hope this book will meet your needs and those of your clients.

ACKNOWLEDGEMENTS

I am deeply grateful to the following:

To my husband, Scott, and our three sons, Tom, Billy, and Dan, for putting other things on hold so that I could pursue this mission. Without your patience, love, and support, this book would not have come to fruition. Thank you for supporting me in all of my endeavors. I appreciate all of your suggestions for this book more than you will ever know!

To my mom, for always being there to help with anything. I appreciate all of your encouragement.

To my sister and my friend, Karen, for her significant role in my journey! Thank you for always being there and for sharing in my enthusiasm of energy techniques.

To my extended family and friends, I appreciate having all of you in my life.

To Gary Craig, EFT founder, for so generously teaching this technique and sharing his wisdom in such a way that he has facilitated a transformation in many people's lives.

To Jim Walters, ND, for his love and enthusiasm of all things energy. Thank you for teaching me what I needed to know.

To Carol Tuttle, for inspiring me to set the intention and get this done. Thank you for your great work in energy therapy.

To Roy Curtain, PhD, for sharing his profound knowledge of quantum physics.

To my editor, JoAnne Keltner, for her insightful guidance.

I would also like to thank the team at Digital Legend for all of their support and for giving me this opportunity for getting this information in print.

I am grateful to God and the Universe for putting everything that I needed before me and allowing every part of my life to unfold perfectly to allow this book to happen.

I would also like to thank all of my clients who have put their trust in me. We have made great progress together.

I sincerely thank all of you who have purchased this book for the special children in your life. I applaud you for knowing the value of EFT and for providing children with this essential tool for living a life of joy.

To the children of the world who will benefit from the exercises in this book—it is my honor to help you to tap into your own joy!

INTRODUCTION

Everything in the Universe is energy! Every bit of matter at the quantum level is energy. Every thought is energy. Every emotion is energy.

Energy vibrates at different rates. Negative emotions have very low vibratory rates. Emotions such as anger, fear, and grief cause blockages in our energy system. Not only do these blockages keep us stuck and focused on the negative, they also affect our physical health. This is no secret to Eastern medicine. The Chinese have understood this for thousands of years.

You are responsible for your own health and well being and that of your children until they are ready to take on that responsibility for themselves. To move fully forward in life, to live in true peace with ourselves, we must clear the negative energy blocks.

The techniques in this book will help your child break the emotional connection to unpleasant memories and experiences and prevent those experiences from having negative consequences on their future.

This book is meant to be a practical reference guide to be used regularly. It takes commitment both on your part and that of your child. Living a life of joy is a journey. You will see first hand how quickly your child can overcome emotional patterns. For those who are new to this concept, I believe it will be a fascinating experience.

What Is EFT?

EFT is an acronym for Emotional Freedom Techniques. EFT, or tapping, is an emotional form of acupressure that was developed in the 1990s by *Gary Craig*. The subtle energies that circulate throughout the body, also known as the meridian system, have been largely ignored by Western science. As a result, Western use of energy therapies for emotional and spiritual healing has been limited. With EFT, we consider blocks in these subtle energies to be the main cause of emotional upsets.

It is an effective and powerful modality to access blocked energy simply by tapping on acupressure points.

In effect, the negative emotions are released and replaced with positive emotions. For most of my clients, this procedure is life changing. Most people feel significant improvement immediately. EFT is safe and easy to learn.

Why Did I Write this Book?

There are two main reasons why I wrote this book.

First, I have seen many lives transformed with EFT. I have facilitated hundreds of sessions that have changed people's lives. I have witnessed my own children excel in many areas using this technique.

I believe that every person in the world will benefit significantly from using EFT. If I could only turn back time, I know how different my childhood would have been if I had this tool at my fingertips. We can all remember how it felt to be afraid of the boogieman or monster in our closet or under our bed. How much time did we waste lying in bed worrying about something that was never even there? We know how it felt if a classmate made fun of us. Often, we never quite trusted them again. We carried those injuries with us for a long time. Many of my adult clients have carried issues from elementary school into their adult lives. Approximately 30% of my adult clients end up clearing at least one issue from elementary school during their first visit. Many times there are family issues that need to be cleared from that stage of life, but so often they need to clear things that a teacher or classmate said to them in order to be free of their current emotional patterns. I have seen senior citizens come to tears telling a story about a grade school teacher who told them they would never amount to anything. While we adapt and move on, often times these emotional scars stay with us forever because we never clear the negative emotional connection associated with the event. Over time, this takes its toll on us and often manifests in physical health consequences. Life is short. The time we have is precious. We have all spent too much time worrying about and dealing with things that can easily and quickly be resolved with EFT. It is critical that we clear the negative emotions, forgive ourselves, forgive others, and move on.

The more I saw the true power of the tool, the more I wanted to help "fix" everyone. What better way to make a difference in the world than to start with our children. With this tool, and the ability to clear these issues as they arise, we spare our children from having to carry any baggage at all. I realized that I personally could not see every child who needed help. Even if I were to see clients around the clock, it would be an impossible feat. I decided that the only way that I could reach more children was to write this book. Every child deserves to have a way to release negativity from their being.

Second, I want to ensure that people learn to use the technique properly so that they get the maximum benefit. I have seen people who used EFT on themselves and have failed. They have given up and think it must not work or that they cannot do it on their own. It does work, and it works all the time. As Gary Craig says, it often works where nothing else will. It is sometimes difficult for someone who has not had experience using this technique to fully understand its power. Therefore, I must caution you. You need to carefully consider the consequences of the wording that you choose if you are going to use this technique on your own.

I am a perfect example of what can go wrong. When I first began learning EFT, I eagerly applied it to everything that bothered me. One of the things I used EFT on was "feeling guilty about overeating." Viola! The guilt was gone. Great! Or so I thought. The problem then became that I noticed myself overeating and feeling no guilt or remorse whatsoever. I gained several pounds before I realized what was happening. While I had effectively eliminated the guilt, I certainly did not want to be gaining weight. I should have been tapping on "not being able to control portion sizes", or "not making good food choices" instead of tapping on the emotion of guilt. I present this example for you to have an awareness of the importance of proper application and wording.

There are no coincidences in life, and luckily I have always believed everything happens for a reason. This inspired me to create fail-proof dialogues to address common emotional issues. I began writing dialogues for my clients to do as homework. I wanted to make sure they got it right. I did not want them having any problems with thinking up things to say on their own, only to find similar failures. I then realized that I was spending a lot of time at the end of client's visits preparing dialogues. After spending much time writing the same things over and over, it finally dawned on me to create handouts for my clients. Then I realized that other people could benefit from this work. Each segment in this book has been carefully thought out to eliminate the possibility of any such failures.

We are living in a very exciting time—a time where information is so readily available. There is no reason that someone in these times should be without this tool. I have seen a number of great books on EFT but not one that specifically addresses children's issues and contains fail-proof dialogues. So, I was inspired to write this book. I wrote the entire book, secured the editors, reviewers and publisher in four weeks. It is amazing what can happen when you work in harmony with the energy of the Universe.

Message to Parents

This book is intended to help you facilitate/guide your child to overcome the everyday minor traumas of childhood life using EFT. While the topics chosen for this book were compiled for the age group of toddlers through teenagers, all of the segments can be used for adults. They will work just as effectively for adults as they do for children. EFT is most effective when it is used on a regular basis. I recommend getting in the routine of doing at least one segment every day. It takes only two to three minutes to complete one segment.

If you do not see a significant decrease in the intensity of the problem, consider seeing an EFT practitioner. This person will be able to work through the issue and determine any underlying causes.

This book is not intended to be used exclusively in a situation where your child has a serious issue. I highly recommend seeing a trained EFT practitioner for any significant fears, phobias, traumas, abuse, compulsions, or chronic emotional issues. If necessary, also seek attention from your medical doctor or licensed psychotherapist.

CHAPTER 1

HOW TO USE THIS BOOK

This book is designed as a step-by-step guide. It contains sixty-one segments related to the issues that I have seen most commonly in my private practice. The segments have been categorized into six chapters. The chapters include confidence/limiting beliefs, family and home, fears, school, transportation, and other emotions and issues.

I encourage you to first talk with your child. Then, review the Table of Contents to determine which segment you feel would best serve your child. If you are uncertain or if several segments seem appropriate, do them all. There is no harm or danger in overdoing EFT.

Open to the segment that you wish to begin working on. Follow the six simple steps that include: rate the intensity, set up, negative taps, forgiving, positive taps, and rate the intensity. There is also a homework assignment at the end of each segment.

Rate the Intensity

In this section, you will rate the intensity of the problem as indicated on the Rate the Intensity scale. At the beginning of each segment, ask your child to think about the problem for a moment. Then have your child rate how much of that emotion they feel on a scale from zero to ten. Zero is no emotional charge, and ten is the most emotional charge that your child can imagine. Younger children may not be able to assign a number to it. That is OK. Have your child point to a place on the scale or have your child hold the palms of their hands together (as in prayer position) for something that is not bothering them and far apart for something that creates a lot of emotional charge or distress. The farther apart they hold their hands, the more it is bothering them. Again, it is not critical to be perfect. You are merely trying to determine where your child is so that when you return to this step after completing the technique, you can see if your child has made progress.

The Tapping Points

The points that you and your child will be tapping on are meridian acupressure points. Review the Tapping Points Diagram to familiarize yourself with the location of the points and their abbreviations. The abbreviations for the points are listed with the dialogue. A diagram of these points accompanies each segment.

When you and your child are tapping, use your index and middle fingers of your dominant hand. It does not matter which side of your face or body you tap on. Tap firmly on each point five to ten times. Tap or pat hard enough to just barely be able to hear the tapping, not hard enough to hurt or cause bruising. Do not be overly concerned about tapping on the exact point. As you tap, you create a percussion that will hit the point if you are not directly on it. You are merely trying to stimulate the acupressure point. You will be coordinating the tapping on the points with the dialogue. It may seem a little awkward at first but after the first couple of rounds, it will become second nature. The following table lists and describes the tapping points.

Table 1 Description of the tapping points and their locations.

Tapping Point and Abbreviation	Description
Karate Chop (KC)	The fleshy part of the side of the hand between the pinkie finger and the wrist.
Eyebrow (EB)	Located directly on top of the eyebrow on the inside edge.
Side of Eye (SE)	Located on the outside edge of the eye. It is on the bone just outside of the eye socket. It is located between the eye and the temple.
Under Eye (UE)	Located on the cheek bone just below the center of the eye.
Under Nose (UN)	Located halfway between the bottom of the nose and the upper lip.
Chin (CH)	Located beneath the lips and just above the chin.

Collarbone (CB)	Located on the innermost part of your collarbone and just to the side of the throat.
Under Arm (UA)	Located on the side of the torso and a few inches below the armpit. It is just below the area that may be ticklish.
Top of Head (TH)	Tap with two or more fingers right in the center of the top of your head.

For ease of finding these points, please refer to the Tapping Points Diagram that follows. A diagram of the tapping points accompanies each segment of the book.

Tapping Points Diagram

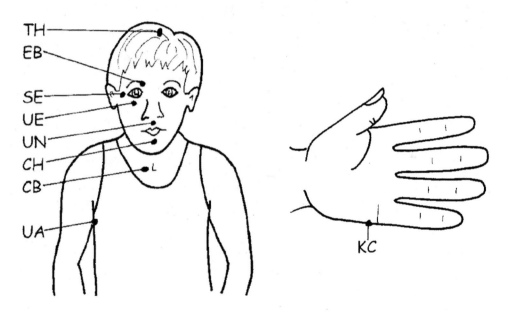

The Set Up

Our bodies adapt to the energy of the negative emotion. That is why we often feel stuck in the negative patterns that we hold onto. The mind is resistant to change. The "even though" statements address this resistance in a very subtle way.

You will continuously tap on the KC, or karate chop point while repeating the three "even though" dialogue statements. A diagram of this point accompanies each segment.

If there is a blank (_____) anywhere in the segment, please fill it in with the word or name that seems most appropriate for your child. You may also wish to make changes in the dialogues in order to make the statement more appropriate to your child's individual need.

For toddlers through 4 years of age: You will read each statement out loud and have your child repeat it the best they can. If they cannot repeat after you, read it out loud and let them tap along. It is also OK if your child does not understand the meaning of every word or phrase in the statements. It will work anyway. If they are unable to tap along, you may tap on them. You will use your index and middle finger of your dominant hand to tap on the tapping points on your child. Tap gently five to ten times on each point. It does not matter which side you tap on.

For ages 5 to 8 years of age: I recommend you tap on your own points and have your child tap on their own points. You will read each statement out loud and have your child repeat the statement. In essence, you will work with them in a follow-the-leader fashion.

For ages 8 years of age through teenagers: I recommend working through a few examples with them so that you are sure they understand the protocol and see the results. Then turn them loose with the book. As much as we would like to think that our children share everything with us, we unfortunately know that this is not true. Kids will be more apt to work on segments on their own that they are not comfortable sharing. For instance, a teenage boy may not want to openly admit that he is afraid of the dark. Once he understands the process, he can clear this problem on his own without having to share it. Most kids feel the need to keep many of the things they are struggling with to themselves. This book is a perfect way for them to be able to address the issues in their own way. This honors them and their privacy. It also provides them the opportunity to master the EFT skills so that they can use this tool throughout their lifetime.

For adults: Simply select a segment that you wish to work on and follow the steps. Correcting your own energy imbalances will not only have positive consequences for you, but will also positively influence your relationships with others. This book is also a wonderful tool for clearing inner child issues.

The Negative Taps

In this step you will be acknowledging the negative aspects of the problem so that you can release them from the energy system.

For the Negative Taps you will be verbalizing the negative aspects of the problem while you are tapping on the tapping points. Again, you will be tapping with the index and middle finger of your dominant hand five to ten times on each point while you say the corresponding statements. It does not matter which side you tap on. Tap on whichever side feels more natural to you and your child. Begin tapping on the EB or eyebrow point while saying the first statement. Then, move down the points while saying the corresponding statements.

The Forgiving Step

The Forgiving Step is very important. In this step, your child will forgive him/herself and the people or the events involved. We all know that we cannot change past circumstances, so we must forgive in order to move on. If we do not forgive, we stay stuck in negative emotional patterns. This is obviously not good to our physical or emotional well-being. This is the step that sets us free.

In the Forgiving Step, you can hold or press the palm of your hand over your heart, gently pat the center of the chest, or rub the center of the chest. You will repeat the statements of forgiveness out loud while you have your child repeat after you.

The Positive Taps

The Positive Taps are essentially affirmation statements that replace the Negative Taps. In many forms of energy therapy, this is known as reframing. Reframing changes the way we perceive our issues. We will be replacing the negative energy by tapping in positive, healthy energy. This will empower your child.

In the Positive Taps section, you and your child will tap on some of the same points and use the same format as for the Negative Taps.

Rate the Intensity

This is my favorite part of the entire process. I love seeing the delight on my clients' faces after tapping away their issues.

In this step, you will follow the same format as you do at the beginning of the process. When you ask your child to rate the intensity of the problem, the intensity will most likely have decreased significantly. If it has not decreased to a zero or a one on the intensity scale, repeat the segment. In many cases, the energy will shift and a different emotion will surface. In this case, you may want to review the Table of Contents and work on another segment of the book.

Homework

The homework will vary according to the segment on which you are working. The most important thing to keep in mind is that you want to have your child repeat the segment daily until you are sure they have resolved the problem.

Final Word

I encourage you to tap along with your child. You will both benefit! Once you start using this guide, it will become increasingly easier to use. Do not worry about perfecting every part of the process immediately. It takes time. This guide is designed to be used routinely. The segments appear redundant. This was done intentionally so that the process becomes second nature. Encourage your children to tap often. We are all constantly being bombarded by negative thoughts, emotions, and outside influences. Tapping helps to neutralize all of the negativity. It should become a life long process.

Often as you work through one issue, other issues surface. Repeat the exercises daily for about three weeks to fully clear the primary issue, any secondary issues, and retrain the energy. If your child is not making progress, please take them to a qualified practitioner. Your child deserves to be free of these problems.

After you and your child have cleared all the major issues, I recommend that you implement a bedtime routine with your child. Encourage your child to talk about their concerns and to express their feelings. Some children may be reluctant to initiate such conversations, so you may need to prompt them. Ask your child if anything that happened during the day is bothering them. Select a segment or two to work on. You can even tap on the tapping points while your child is telling you the story. Next, ask your child to tell you about the best things that happened during the day. Then, ask your child to state two or three things for which they are grateful. This routine is a great way to spend quality time together and is a wonderful way to end the day.

CHAPTER 2

CONFIDENCE/LIMITING BELIEFS

It is very difficult for a child to thrive when they are stuck in patterns of limiting beliefs. The segments in this chapter relate to confidence and self-image. These segments will help your child to break undesirable habits, improve performance, empower them to make good decisions, and improve self esteem.

Have your child repeat the segments regularly to replace these negative patterns with positive emotional patterns.

Confidence/Limiting Beliefs

Segments Presented in This Chapter

Bad Habit
Being Bullied
Being Made Fun Of
Do Not Like to Be Apart or Separated
Food Choices
I Cannot Do It
I Do Not Fit In
I Look Different
Making a Mistake
Not Good Enough
Peer Pressure
Potty Training
Someone Hurt My Feelings
Staying in My Bed
Tapping Doesn't Work

Bad Habit

1. Rate the Intensity

Select on a scale of 0 to 10 how much you want or need to repeat this habit, with 10 being the most intense and 0 being not at all.

0	1	2	3	4	5	6	7	8	9	10

2. Set up

Keep tapping the karate chop point the whole time as you say the following:

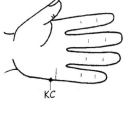

Even though I have this bad habit,
I am an awesome kid.
Even though I am afraid I will never be able to quit _____,
I am a great person.
Even though I won't be OK without this habit, I am a good person.

3. Negative Taps

Tap down the points as you say the following:

EB: I cannot stop it.
SE: I will never be able to stop.
UE: It is not safe for me to stop.
UN: I need to _____.
CH: What will I do if I cannot _____?
CB: I have to _____.
UA: I will never be able to break this habit.
TH: All of the left over feelings that I cannot stop my habit.

Stop tapping.

Take in a super big breath and then blow out all of the air.

4. Forgiving

Hold your hand over your heart as you say the following:

I forgive myself for having this habit; I am doing the best I can.
I forgive myself for not knowing how to stop it; I am doing my best.

Take in another super big breath and then blow out all of the air.

5. Positive Taps

Tap down the points as you say the following:

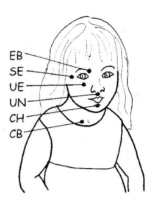

EB: I am letting go of this habit.
SE: I do not need this habit.
UE: I do not need to _____ anymore.
UN: I am safe without this habit.
CH: I am ready to change.
CB: I am happy and proud of myself.

6. Rate the Intensity

Select on a scale of 0 to 10 how much you want or feel you need to repeat this habit, with 10 being the most intense and 0 being not at all.

0	1	2	3	4	5	6	7	8	9	10

Homework

Repeat this process two or more times every day for three weeks.
Repeat this process any time you feel the need to go back to your old habit.

Being Bullied

1. Rate the Intensity

Select on a scale of 0 to 10 how much it bothers you to feel bullied, with 10 being the most intense and 0 being not at all.

0	1	2	3	4	5	6	7	8	9	10

2. Set up

Keep tapping the karate chop point the whole time as you say the following:

KC

> Even though I feel bullied,
> I love and accept myself.
> Even though someone acted tough and it made me feel weak, I am an awesome kid.
> Even though someone tried to control me, I am great just the way I am.

3. Negative Taps

Tap down the points as you say the following:

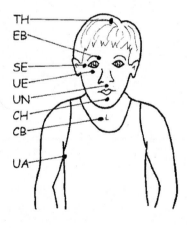

> EB: I feel bullied.
> SE: Someone bullied me.
> UE: People are always pushing me around.
> UN: I feel like I have to give in to them.
> CH: I cannot stand up for myself.
> CB: I let them get my power.
> UA: Feeling bullied.
> TH: All of the left over fear of being bullied.

Stop tapping.

Take in a super big breath and then blow out all of the air.

4. Forgiving

Hold your hand over your heart as you say the following:

> I forgive myself for letting someone bully me; I did the best I knew how.
> I forgive them for bullying me; they do not know any better.

Take in another super big breath and then blow out all of the air.

5. Positive Taps

Tap down the points as you say the following:

> EB: I am letting go of this fear.
> I am forgiving myself.
> SE: I can let it go.
> I won't allow it to happen anymore.
> UE: I can stand up for myself.
> I can do what is right.
> UN: I can make good choices. I can be proud of myself.
> CH: I do not feel worried.
> CB: I am free from feeling bullied now and forever.

6. Rate the Intensity

Select on a scale of 0 to 10 how much it bothers you to feel bullied, with 10 being the most intense and 0 being not at all.

0	1	2	3	4	5	6	7	8	9	10

Homework

Close your eyes. Take some deep breaths. Imagine that you are in a situation where you would normally feel bullied. Imagine yourself feeling completely safe and in control. Take a minute and enjoy the feeling of safety all around your body.

Being Made Fun Of

1. Rate the Intensity

Select on a scale of 0 to 10 how much it bothers you to be made fun of, with 10 being the most intense and 0 being not at all.

0	1	2	3	4	5	6	7	8	9	10

2. Set up

Keep tapping the karate chop point the whole time as you say the following:

KC

Even though _____ made fun of me,
I am a good person.
Even though someone is always making fun of me, I am an awesome kid.
Even though they make fun of me, I accept who I am.

3. Negative Taps

Tap down the points as you say the following:

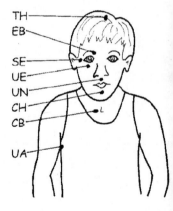
TH
EB
SE
UE
UN
CH
CB
UA
L

EB: I do not like being made fun of.
SE: It makes me sad.
UE: It hurts my feelings. Whatever they said must be true.
UN: It makes me mad.
CH: I can never forget this. I will never forgive them.
CB: Other kids laugh about it. I cannot trust them.
UA: I thought they were my friends.
TH: All of the left over fear of someone making fun of me.

Stop tapping.

Take in a super big breath and then blow out all of the air.

4. Forgiving

Hold your hand over your heart as you say the following:

I forgive myself for being made fun of; I am doing the best I can.
I forgive those who made fun of me; they do not know any better.

Take in another super big breath and then blow out all of the air.

5. Positive Taps

Tap down the points as you say
the following:

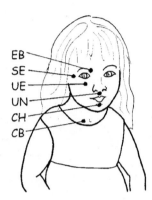

EB: I am letting go of the sadness.
SE: I can forgive them.
UE: I do not need to feel mad anymore.
UN: I am strong and brave.
CH: I am healed. I feel joy.
CB: I can stand up for myself in a good way.

6. Rate the Intensity

Select on a scale of 0 to 10 how much it bothers you to think about being made fun of, with 10 being the most intense and 0 being not at all.

0	1	2	3	4	5	6	7	8	9	10

Homework

Repeat this process every day for a few weeks. You can repeat this any time you feel upset that someone made fun of you.

Do Not Like to Be Apart or Separated

1. Rate the Intensity

Select on a scale of 0 to 10 how much you dislike being apart, with 10 being the most intense and 0 being not at all.

0	1	2	3	4	5	6	7	8	9	10

2. Set up

Keep tapping the karate chop point the whole time as you say the following:

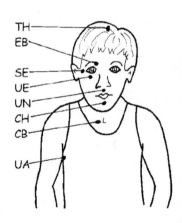

Even though I do not like to be apart from _____, I love myself.
Even though I feel lonely and I miss _____, I am a good person.
Even though I am sad to be apart, I am an awesome kid.

3. Negative Taps

Tap down the points as you say the following:

EB: I do not like being separated.
SE: Why do I have to go?
Why do they have to go?
UE: Why can't _____ stay?
UN: It feels sad.
CH: I am lonely without _____.
CB: I miss _____. What if _____ doesn't come back?
UA: I am afraid.
TH: All of the left over sad feelings.

Stop tapping.

Take in a super big breath and then blow out all of the air.

4. Forgiving
Hold your hand over your heart as you say the following:

I forgive myself for not wanting to be apart; I am doing my best.

I forgive _____ for leaving me; he/she is doing the best he/she knows how.

Take in another super big breath and then blow out all of the air.

5. Positive Taps
Tap down the points as you say the following:

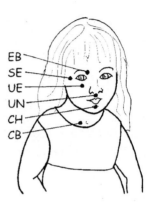

EB: I am letting all the bad feelings go away.

SE: I know _____ will come back for me.

UE: I can have fun with other people.

UN: It is good to make new friends.

CH: I am safe and comfortable. I feel joy.

CB: I am free from feeling lonely and worried.

6. Rate the Intensity
Select on a scale of 0 to 10 how much you dislike being apart or separated, with 10 being the most intense and 0 being not at all.

0	1	2	3	4	5	6	7	8	9	10

Homework
Repeat this anytime you are sad and will need to be apart from someone you love. Note to parents: If your child continues to suffer from separation anxiety after doing this process, please consider taking them to an EFT practitioner or energy therapist.

Food Choices

1. Rate the Intensity
Select on a scale of 0 to 10 how hard it is for you to make good food choices, with 10 being the most intense and 0 being not at all.

0	1	2	3	4	5	6	7	8	9	10

2. Set up
Keep tapping the karate chop point the whole time as you say the following:

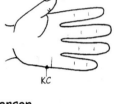

KC

Even though it is hard to make good food choices, I am a good person.
Even though junk food is hard to resist, I am a very good person.
Even though I make bad food choices, I am proud of myself.

3. Negative Taps
Tap down the points as you say the following:

EB: I cannot make good choices.
SE: I do not like the way healthy foods taste.
UE: Healthy food is too blah.
UN: All of my friends eat junk food. They might make fun of me if I do not eat it.
CH: Junk food tastes good.
CB: I do not care if it is not good for me.
UA: I do not care if I am not healthy.
TH: All of the left over bad food choices.

Stop tapping.

Take in a super big breath and then blow out all of the air.

4. Forgiving
Hold your hand over your heart as you say the following:

> I forgive myself for not making good food choices; I have done my best and I know that it is important for me to make good choices now.

Take in another super big breath and then blow out all of the air.

5. Positive Taps
Tap down the points as you say the following:

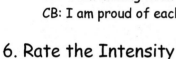

> EB: I am learning a lot about food.
> I am aware of what I am eating.
> SE: Healthy food makes my body strong.
> UE: I will make good food choices.
> I am choosing to drink water instead of pop.
> UN: Fruit is good. Vegetables are good.
> CH: I am making healthy choices. My body thanks me for my good choices.
> CB: I am proud of each of my healthy food choices!

6. Rate the Intensity
Select on a scale of 0 to 10 how hard it is for you to make good food choices, with 10 being the most intense and 0 being not at all.

0	1	2	3	4	5	6	7	8	9	10

Homework
Repeat this process two times every day until you notice yourself making healthier food choices. Repeat this process any time you notice that you are getting in the habit of eating junk food. Be aware of what you are eating and how it affects your body.

I Cannot Do It

1. Rate the Intensity

Select on a scale of 0 to 10 how strongly you feel you cannot do it, with 10 being the most intense and 0 being not at all.

0	1	2	3	4	5	6	7	8	9	10

2. Set up

Keep tapping the karate chop point the whole time as you say the following:

Even though I feel I cannot do it, I am an awesome kid.
Even though I do not think I can do it, I am the best person ever.
Even though I think I cannot do it, I am smart and will find a way.

3. Negative Taps

Tap down the points as you say the following:

EB: I cannot do it!
SE: I will never be able to do it.
UE: It is just too hard.
UN: It is impossible.
CH: I cannot.
CB: I won't even try.
UA: I'll never be able to do it.
TH: All of the left over feelings that I cannot do it.

Stop tapping.

Take in a super big breath and then blow out all of the air.

4. Forgiving
Hold your hand over your heart as you say the following:

I forgive myself for thinking I cannot do it; I am doing my best and I know I can.

I forgive myself for not having confidence and thinking it would be too hard.

Take in another super big breath and then blow out all of the air.

5. Positive Taps
Tap down the points as you say the following:

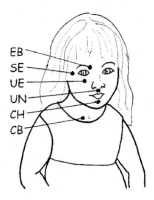

EB: I am no longer afraid of not being able to do it.

SE: I can do it. I have confidence!

UE: I can find a way.

UN: I can figure it out.

CH: I can try my best.

CB: I think I can. I know I can. I will do it!

6. Rate the Intensity
Select on a scale of 0 to 10 how strongly you feel that you cannot do it, with 10 being the most intense and 0 being not at all.

0	1	2	3	4	5	6	7	8	9	10

Homework
Repeat this process two to three times per day until you know in your heart that you can do it. Know that you can achieve anything you set out to accomplish. Close your eyes for a moment and picture yourself succeeding.

I Do Not Fit In

1. Rate the Intensity

Select on a scale of 0 to 10 how strongly you feel you do not fit in, with 10 being the most intense and 0 being not at all.

0	1	2	3	4	5	6	7	8	9	10

2. Set up

Keep tapping the karate chop point the whole time as you say the following:

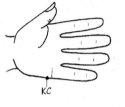

Even though I do not fit in, I love myself.
Even though I do not feel like everyone else, I am a good person.
Even though nobody pays attention to me, I am an awesome friend.

3. Negative Taps

Tap down the points as you say the following:

EB: I do not fit in.
SE: Nobody likes me.
UE: I worry about what other people think of me.
UN: Everyone pays a lot of attention to what I say and do.
CH: I worry about what I should say.
CB: I worry about what I should do.
UA: I cannot be myself.
TH: All of the left over feeling like I do not fit in.

Stop tapping.
Take in a super big breath and then blow out all of the air.

4. Forgiving
Hold your hand over your heart as you say the following:

> I forgive myself for not feeling like I fit in; I am doing the best I know how.
> I forgive everyone who makes me feel like I do not fit in; they are doing their best.

Take in another super big breath and then blow out all of the air.

5. Positive Taps
Tap down the points as you say the following:

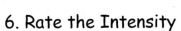

> EB: I am letting go of this feeling. I do not need to please everyone.
> SE: I can be free of all the thinking and worrying.
> UE: I am perfect just the way I am.
> UN: I am thinking for myself.
> CH: I do fit in. I am happy and grateful for who I am.
> CB: I am comfortable being who I am.

6. Rate the Intensity
Select on a scale of 0 to 10 how strongly you feel that you do not fit in, with 10 being the most intense and 0 being not at all.

0	1	2	3	4	5	6	7	8	9	10

Homework
Repeat this process a couple times per day until you feel good about yourself. You should always feel comfortable being yourself.

I Look Different

1. Rate the Intensity

Select on a scale of 0 to 10 how much it bothers you that you feel you look different, with 10 being the most intense and 0 being not at all.

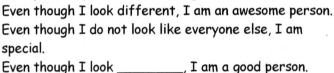

0	1	2	3	4	5	6	7	8	9	10

2. Set up

Keep tapping the karate chop point the whole time as you say the following:

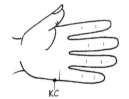

KC

Even though I look different, I am an awesome person.
Even though I do not look like everyone else, I am special.
Even though I look _____, I am a good person.

3. Negative Taps

Tap down the points as you say the following:

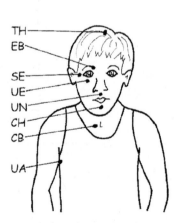

TH
EB
SE
UE
UN
CH
CB
UA

EB: I am different.
SE: I am not normal.
UE: Other kids do not like me because I am different.
UN: Kids make fun of me.
CH: They hurt my feelings and make me sad.
CB: I am not OK.
UA: I look different and that doesn't feel right.
TH: All of the left over feelings about looking different.

Stop tapping.
Take in a super big breath and then blow out all of the air.

4. Forgiving
Hold your hand over your heart as you say the following:

> I forgive myself for looking different; I am special and perfect.
> I forgive other people for the way they look; everyone is special in their own way.
> I forgive other people for making me feel different; they are doing the best they know how.

Take in another super big breath and then blow out all of the air.

5. Positive Taps
Tap down the points as you say the following:

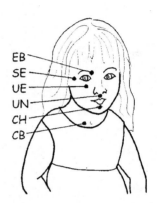

> EB: I am letting go of feeling like being different is a bad thing.
> SE: I can feel good about myself.
> UE: I am OK just the way I am.
> UN: I am safe and comfortable.
> CH: I am free from feeling different.
> CB: I feel good about how I look.

6. Rate the Intensity
Select on a scale of 0 to 10 how much it bothers you that you feel you look different, with 10 being the most intense and 0 being not at all.

0	1	2	3	4	5	6	7	8	9	10

Homework
Repeat this process every day for a few weeks so that you can retrain your energy. Note to parents: Please see a qualified therapist for deeper issues related to your child's self image.

Making a Mistake

1. Rate the Intensity
Select on a scale of 0 to 10 how much it bothers you to make a mistake, with 10 being the most intense and 0 being not at all.

0	1	2	3	4	5	6	7	8	9	10

2. Set up
Keep tapping the karate chop point the whole time as you say the following:

KC

> Even though I made a mistake, I am a good person.
> Even though I am afraid of making another mistake, I am an awesome kid.
> Even though I make mistakes, I am the best person ever.

3. Negative Taps
Tap down the points as you say the following:

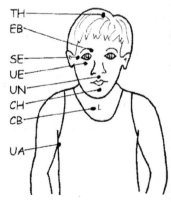

> EB: I made a mistake.
> SE: I made a big mistake.
> UE: I didn't mean to do it.
> UN: I feel bad that I made a mistake.
> CH: I never want to do that again.
> CB: It was bad. I feel embarrassed. I feel foolish.
> UA: It was a big mistake.
> TH: All of the left over bad feelings about making a mistake.

Stop tapping.

Take in a super big breath and then blow out all of the air.

4. Forgiving

Hold your hand over your heart as you say the following:

I forgive myself for making that mistake; I have learned not to do it again.
I forgive myself for being afraid of making another mistake; I am doing my best.

Take in another super big breath and then blow out all of the air.

5. Positive Taps

Tap down the points as you say the following:

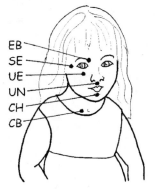

EB: Everyone has made mistakes.
SE: I can forgive myself.
UE: I can let it go.
UN: I can let go of feeling bad about making that mistake.
CH: I have learned from my mistake.
CB: I feel OK now. I am happy and proud of myself.

6. Rate the Intensity

Select on a scale of 0 to 10 how much it bothers you to think about making a mistake, with 10 being the most intense and 0 being not at all.

0	1	2	3	4	5	6	7	8	9	10

Homework
Repeat this process until you forgive yourself for making the mistake.

Not Good Enough

1. Rate the Intensity
Select on a scale of 0 to 10 how strongly you feel that you are not good enough, with 10 being the most intense and 0 being not at all.

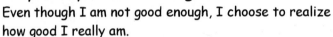

2. Set up
Keep tapping the karate chop point the whole time as you say the following:

    Even though I am not good enough, I choose to realize how good I really am.
    Even though I am not good at _____, I am an awesome person.
    Even though I am not as good as _____, I am a smart person.

3. Negative Taps
Tap down the points as you say the following:

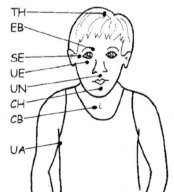

    EB: I am not good enough.
    SE: Everyone else does it better than me.
    UE: I feel worthless.
    UN: I am not good at _____.
    CH: I cannot get any better at it.
    CB: I will never get any better.
    UA: I will never be good enough.
    TH: All of the left over feelings of not being good enough.

Stop tapping.
Take in a super big breath and then blow out all of the air.

4. Forgiving
Hold your hand over your heart as you say the following:

I forgive myself for not feeling like I am good enough; I am doing my best.
I forgive myself for not being good enough; I am doing the best I know how.
I forgive others who make me feel like I am not as good as them; they are doing their best too!

Take in another super big breath and then blow out all of the air.

5. Positive Taps
Tap down the points as you say the following:

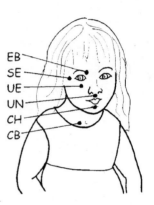

EB: I am letting go of not feeling good enough.
SE: I can let it go forever.
UE: I am good at everything I do.
UN: I try my hardest, and I do a good job.
CH: I know I can improve.
CB: I get better all the time. It is easy and fun.

6. Rate the Intensity
Select on a scale of 0 to 10 how strongly you feel you are not good enough, with 10 being the most intense and 0 being not at all.

0	1	2	3	4	5	6	7	8	9	10

Homework
Repeat this process every day until you notice yourself being as good at _____ as you wish to be.

Peer Pressure

1. Rate the Intensity

Select on a scale of 0 to 10 how much peer pressure you feel, with 10 being the most intense and 0 being not at all.

0	1	2	3	4	5	6	7	8	9	10

2. Set up

Keep tapping the karate chop point the whole time as you say the following:

Even though _____ makes me feel like I do not fit in, I am an awesome kid.
Even though I feel a lot of pressure to do what other people are doing, I am able to make my own decisions.
Even though I feel like I have to please them, I am perfect the way I am.

3. Negative Taps

Tap down the points as you say the following:

EB: This really hurts my feelings!
SE: I am being pulled in two different directions.
UE: I am afraid they won't like me. I am sad. What will I do if they do not like me?
UN: Why does _____ think I have to do this?
CH: I do not like when I feel this way. What if people make fun of me?
CB: If _____ wants me to change, then he/she doesn't like me.
UA: I feel like I need to change myself to fit in.
TH: All of the left over pressure that I am feeling.

Stop tapping.

Take in a super big breath and then blow out all of the air.

4. Forgiving
Hold your hand over your heart as you say the following:

> I forgive myself for feeling this peer pressure; I am doing the best I can.
> I forgive _____ for trying to persuade me; _____ doesn't know any better.

Take in another super big breath and then blow out all of the air.

5. Positive Taps
Tap down the points as you say the following:

> EB: I am no longer feeling hurt.
> I am not afraid anymore.
> SE: I am letting all of the pressure go.
> I will get through this.
> UE: I know that I do not have to change myself to please others. I can think for myself.
> UN: I know that I am perfect just the way I am. I am happy.
> CH: It feels good to be happy. I know that I am doing what is right for me.
> CB: I trust my gut-feelings. I am happy and free! I feel joyful.

6. Rate the Intensity
Select on a scale of 0 to 10 how much peer pressure you feel, with 10 being the most intense and 0 being not at all.

0	1	2	3	4	5	6	7	8	9	10

Homework
Repeat this process as many times as you need to until you feel better. You should never do anything that doesn't feel right. Always trust your judgment.

Potty Training

1. Rate the Intensity
Select on a scale of 0 to 10 how hard it is for you to go to the bathroom when you need to, with 10 being the most intense and 0 being not at all.

0	1	2	3	4	5	6	7	8	9	10

2. Set up
Keep tapping the karate chop point the whole time as you say the following:

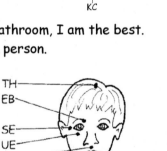

> Even though I do not go on the potty,
> I am an awesome kid.
> Even though I do not think I can make it to the bathroom, I am the best.
> Even though I do not want to change, I am a good person.

3. Negative Taps
Tap down the points as you say the following:

> EB: I cannot do it!
> SE: I will never be able to make it to the bathroom in time.
> UE: It is just too hard. What if I have an accident?
> UN: I do not want to grow-up. I like my pull-ups/training pants/diapers.
> CH: I do not want to try. What if I am left alone for too long?
> CB: I won't even try. I'll never be able to do it. The toilet is scary.
> UA: I am afraid that I might fall in. What if the water gets on me? It makes me feel yucky.
> TH: All of the left over feelings that I cannot go on the potty.

Stop tapping.
Take in a super big breath and then blow out all of the air.

4. Forgiving

Hold your hand over your heart as you say the following:

> I forgive myself for thinking I cannot do it; I know I can.
> I forgive myself for thinking it would be too hard; I am doing my best.
> I forgive myself for not wanting to do it; I am doing the best I can.

Take in another super big breath and then blow out all of the air.

5. Positive Taps

Tap down the points as you say the following:

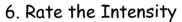

> EB: I am no longer afraid to do it.
> SE: I can do it. I have confidence!
> UE: I will know when I need to go to the bathroom.
> UN: I will be able to make it to the bathroom.
> CH: I can try my best. I am proud that I go on the potty.
> CB: I know I can. I will show everyone that I am a big boy/girl!

6. Rate the Intensity

Select on a scale of 0 to 10 how hard it is for you to go to the bathroom when you need to, with 10 being the most intense and 0 being not at all.

0	1	2	3	4	5	6	7	8	9	10

Homework

Repeat this process two to three times per day until you know that you can do it.
Note to parents: Substitute any words that your child is more comfortable using.

Someone Hurt My Feelings

1. Rate the Intensity
Select on a scale of 0 to 10 how much it bothers you that someone hurt your feelings, with 10 being the most intense and 0 being not at all.

0	1	2	3	4	5	6	7	8	9	10

2. Set up
Keep tapping the karate chop point the whole time as you say the following:

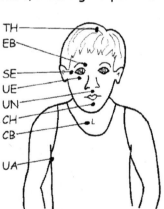

KC

>Even though _____ hurt my feelings,
>I am an awesome kid.
>Even though I think he/she did it on purpose, I am the best.
>Even though I do not like it when my feelings are hurt, I am a good person.

3. Negative Taps
Tap down the points as you say the following:

>EB: _____ hurt my feelings!
>SE: It makes me sad.
>UE: It hurts so much.
>UN: I do not know why he/she did it.
>CH: I do not like when I feel this way.
>It feels really bad.
>CB: If _____ hurt my feelings then it makes
>me afraid he/she doesn't like me. What is wrong with me?
>UA: What is wrong with _____? Why doesn't he/she like me?
>TH: All of the left over sadness that _____ hurt my feelings.

Stop tapping.

Take in a super big breath and then blow out all of the air.

4. Forgiving
Hold your hand over your heart as you say the following:

I forgive my feelings for being hurt; I am doing the best I can.

I forgive _____ for hurting my feelings; _____ is doing his/her best.

Take in another super big breath and then blow out all of the air.

5. Positive Taps
Tap down the points as you say the following:

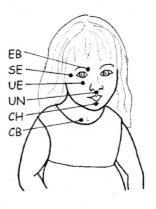

EB: I am no longer feeling hurt.
I am not afraid anymore.
SE: I am letting all of the hurt feelings go away.
UE: I feel happy now.
UN: I feel much better.
CH: It feels good to be happy.
CB: I am happy and free!

6. Rate the Intensity
Select on a scale of 0 to 10 how much it bothers you that someone hurt your feelings, with 10 being the most intense and 0 being not at all.

0	1	2	3	4	5	6	7	8	9	10

Homework
Repeat this process two to three times until you feel better.

Staying in My Bed

1. Rate the Intensity
Select on a scale of 0 to 10 how difficult it is for you to stay in your bed, with 10 being the most intense and 0 being not at all.

0	1	2	3	4	5	6	7	8	9	10

2. Set up
Keep tapping the karate chop point the whole time as you say the following:

KC

> Even though I do not stay in my bed
> all night, I am an awesome kid.
> Even though I always need to get up, I can break the habit.
> Even though I just cannot stay in my bed all night, I am a good person.

3. Negative Taps
Tap down the points as you say the following:

> EB: It is really hard to stay in my bed.
> SE: There are too many reasons to get up.
> UE: I am scared.
> UN: I am thirsty.
> CH: I do not like being alone.
> CB: I do not want to sleep.
> UA: I do not want to stay in my bed. I cannot do it.
> TH: All of the left over fear of staying in my bed.

Stop tapping.
Take in a super big breath and then blow out all of the air.

4. Forgiving
Hold your hand over your heart as you say the following:

> I forgive myself for not wanting to stay in my bed; I am doing my best.
> I forgive myself for getting out of my bed; I am doing the best I know how.

Take in another super big breath and then blow out all of the air.

5. Positive Taps
Tap down the points as you say the following:

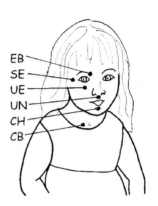

> EB: I am letting go of anything that keeps me from staying in my bed.
> SE: I can stay in my bed all night.
> UE: I can do it!
> UN: I can relax and get a good night's sleep without having to get up.
> CH: I only need to get up to use the bathroom.
> CB: I am proud of myself for staying in my bed.

6. Rate the Intensity
Select on a scale of 0 to 10 how difficult it is for you to stay in your bed, with 10 being the most intense and 0 being not at all.

0	1	2	3	4	5	6	7	8	9	10

Homework
Repeat this process every night for three weeks.

Note to parents: If your child continues to have difficulty after doing this segment, please consider taking them to an EFT practitioner to clear deeper issues.

Tapping Does Not Work

1. Rate the Intensity
Select on a scale of 0 to 10 how strongly you feel that tapping does not work, with 10 being the most intense and 0 being not at all.

0	1	2	3	4	5	6	7	8	9	10

2. Set up
Keep tapping the karate chop point the whole time as you say the following:

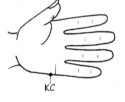
KC

Even though I do not think tapping works,
I am an awesome kid.
Even though I am afraid that tapping will not help me, I know I am good.
Even though I know tapping won't work for me, I am perfect, whole, and complete.

3. Negative Taps
Tap down the points as you say the following:

EB: Tapping does not work.
SE: This is silly.
UE: I do not believe it will work.
UN: How can tapping on myself make me feel better?
CH: I do not think it will work.
CB: It might work for some kids but it will never work for me.
UA: It is impossible for this to help me. My problems are real.
TH: All of the left over fear and doubt that tapping will not work.

Stop tapping.
Take in a super big breath and then blow out all of the air.

4. Forgiving

Hold your hand over your heart as you say the following:

I forgive myself for not trusting this tapping; I am doing my best.

I forgive myself for thinking this won't help me; I am doing the best I know how.

Take in another super big breath and then blow out all of the air.

5. Positive Taps

Tap down the points as you say the following:

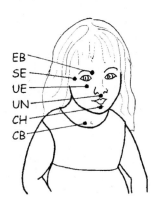

EB: I am letting go of this fear.

SE: I can let go of any doubts.

UE: I will allow this tapping to clear any of my blocked energy.

UN: I am safe and secure.

CH: Tapping is simple and safe.

CB: I am comfortable knowing that tapping works for me.

6. Rate the Intensity

Select on a scale of 0 to 10 how strongly you feel that tapping does not work, with 10 being the most intense and 0 being not at all.

0	1	2	3	4	5	6	7	8	9	10

Homework

Repeat this process until you feel confident to give it a try.

CHAPTER 3

FAMILY AND HOME

The segments in this chapter relate to family and home issues. The segments relate to changes in family structure, relationships within the family, and the dynamics within the home.

If you and your child are experiencing grief over the loss of a family member or the loss of a family pet, please refer to Chapter 7—Other Emotions and Issues.

Family and Home

Segments Presented in This Chapter

Moving
New Baby
Parents Arguing
Parents Are Divorced
Parents Getting Divorced – Fear Of
Problems with Brother or Sister

Moving

1. Rate the Intensity
Select on a scale of 0 to 10 how much the thought of moving bothers you, with 10 being the most intense and 0 being not at all.

0	1	2	3	4	5	6	7	8	9	10

2. Set up
Keep tapping the karate chop point the whole time as you say the following:

KC

> Even though I have to move, I am OK with who I am.
> Even though I do not want to move, I am a good person.
> Even though moving will be hard, I am an awesome kid.

3. Negative Taps
Tap down the points as you say the following:

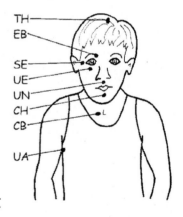

TH
EB
SE
UE
UN
CH
CB
L
UA

> EB: I am afraid I won't make new friends.
> SE: I have to go to a new school (if applicable)
> UE: What if I do not like my new house?
> UN: I will miss this place.
> CH: I will miss my family and friends that will stay here.
> CB: I won't know anyone there.
> UA: I do not want to move. Nobody cares that I do not want to move.
> TH: All of the left over sadness and fear about moving.

Stop tapping.
Take in a super big breath and then blow out all of the air.

4. Forgiving
Hold your hand over your heart as you say the following:

I forgive myself for not wanting to move, I am doing my best.
I forgive my family for making me move; they are doing their best, too.

Take in another super big breath and then blow out all of the air.

5. Positive Taps
Tap down the points as you say
the following:

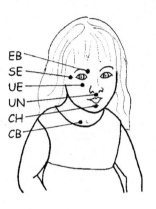

EB: I am feeling better about moving.
SE: I can find fun things to do at
my new house.
UE: I will meet new friends.
UN: Changes are not so bad.
CH: Changes are good. I am excited about moving.
CB: I am letting go of all the bad feelings about
moving, now and forever!

6. Rate the Intensity
Select on a scale of 0 to 10 how much the thought of moving bothers you, with 10 being the most intense and 0 being not at all.

0	1	2	3	4	5	6	7	8	9	10

Homework
Repeat this sequence daily until you feel better about moving.

New Baby

1. Rate the Intensity
Select on a scale of 0 to 10 how much having a new baby in the family bothers you, with 10 being the most intense and 0 being not at all.

0	1	2	3	4	5	6	7	8	9	10

2. Set up
Keep tapping the karate chop point the whole time as you say the following:

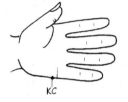

KC

> Even though the new baby gets all of the attention, I am a good person.
> Even though I do not feel special, I am an awesome kid.
> Even though I will have to share my things with the baby, I am a good big brother/sister.

3. Negative Taps
Tap down the points as you say the following:

> EB: Everybody wants to play with our new baby.
> SE: Nobody pays attention to me.
> UE: I do not feel special anymore.
> UN: No one has time for me.
> CH: I always have to help with the baby.
> CB: Nobody is excited to see me.
> UA: I feel jealous and angry.
> TH: All of the left over sad feelings about the new baby.

Stop tapping.

Take in a super big breath and then blow out all of the air.

4. Forgiving
Hold your hand over your heart as you say the following:

> I forgive myself for not feeling happy about the new baby; I am doing my best.
>
> I forgive my family for paying so much attention to the new baby; they are happy for all of us.
>
> I forgive my parents for spending so much time with the baby; they are doing their best.

Take in another super big breath and then blow out all of the air.

5. Positive Taps
Tap down the points as you say the following:

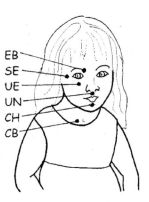

> EB: I am letting go of the sad feelings.
> SE: I can feel happy about the baby.
> UE: I am free from the bad feelings.
> UN: My family loves us all equally.
> CH: I am lucky to have a new baby brother/sister in my family.
> CB: I am special. I am tapping in the joy.

6. Rate the Intensity
Select on a scale of 0 to 10 how much having a new baby in the family bothers you, with 10 being the most intense and 0 being not at all.

0	1	2	3	4	5	6	7	8	9	10

Homework
Repeat this process until you feel better..

Parents Arguing

1. Rate the Intensity
Select on a scale of 0 to 10 how much your parents arguing bothers you, with 10 being the most intense and 0 being not at all.

0	1	2	3	4	5	6	7	8	9	10

2. Set up
Keep tapping the karate chop point the whole time as you say the following:

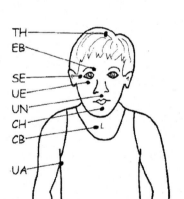

Even though I am afraid because my parents argued, I am a fantastic person.
Even though I am scared that my parents do not like each other, I am an awesome kid.
Even though it is scary to hear them fight, I am a great son/daughter.

3. Negative Taps
Tap down the points as you say the following:

EB: It is hard to see other people get angry.
SE: I am afraid when people yell.
UE: It is scary.
UN: I am afraid that they do not love each other.
CH: I am afraid they do not love me.
CB: I am afraid they will yell at me.
UA: They said mean things to each other.
TH: All of the left over fear and bad feelings about hearing my parents argue.

Stop tapping.
Take in a super big breath and then blow out all of the air.

4. Forgiving
Hold your hand over your heart as you say the following:

I forgive myself for feeling afraid; I am doing the best I can.

I forgive my parents for fighting, getting mad, and saying the things they did; they are doing the best they can.

Take in another super big breath and then blow out all of the air.

5. Positive Taps
Tap down the points as you say the following:

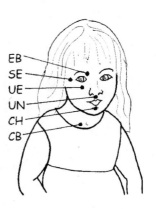

EB: I am safe.

SE: I am happy.

UE: Everything will be OK.

UN: My parents will work it out. They are grown ups, and they can figure it out.

CH: I am no longer afraid. I do not have to worry any more.

CB: I am safe and free to be happy.

6. Rate the Intensity
Select on a scale of 0 to 10 how much your parents arguing bothers you, with 10 being the most intense and 0 being not at all.

0	1	2	3	4	5	6	7	8	9	10

Homework
Repeat this process until you are feeling better.

Parents Are Divorced

1. Rate the Intensity
Select on a scale of 0 to 10 how much your parent's divorce upsets you, with 10 being the most intense and 0 being not at all.

0	1	2	3	4	5	6	7	8	9	10

2. Set up
Keep tapping the karate chop point the whole time as you say the following:

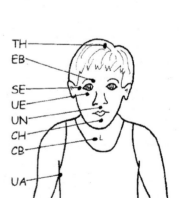

KC

> Even though my parents are divorced, I choose to be happy.
> Even though I do not think my parents like each other, I am an awesome kid.
> Even though mom and dad got divorced, I am a good person.

3. Negative Taps
Tap down the points as you say the following:

> EB: I feel sad. I feel different.
> SE: I do not want my parents to be divorced.
> UE: Other people act different towards me because of the divorce.
> UN: I am afraid it is my fault. It is my fault.
> CH: I am angry. I blame myself. I blame them.
> CB: I do not understand why they had to get divorced.
> UA: I miss the way it was. It will never be the same.
> TH: All of the left over sadness about the divorce.

Stop tapping.

Take in a super big breath and then blow out all of the air.

4. Forgiving

Hold your hand over your heart as you say the following:

I forgive myself for feeling bad; I am doing the best I know how.

I forgive my parents for getting divorced; they always do the best they can.

Take in another super big breath and then blow out all of the air.

5. Positive Taps

Tap down the points as you say the following:

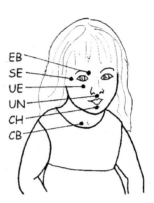

EB: I am safe.

SE: I will be OK. I am loved.

UE: My parents love me.

UN: I am letting go of all the sadness.

CH: It is OK to be with each parent separately.

CB: I am tapping into joy. I am safe and happy.

6. Rate the Intensity

Select on a scale of 0 to 10 how much your parent's divorce upsets you, with 10 being the most intense and 0 being not at all.

0	1	2	3	4	5	6	7	8	9	10

Homework

You may also choose to work on the "Do Not Like being Apart," "Anger," Frustrated," "Guilt," "Sadness," or "Moving" segments of this book.

Parents Getting Divorced – Fear Of

1. Rate the Intensity
Select on a scale of 0 to 10 how afraid you are that your parents will get a divorce, with 10 being the most intense and 0 being not at all.

0	1	2	3	4	5	6	7	8	9	10

2. Set up
Keep tapping the karate chop point the whole time as you say the following:

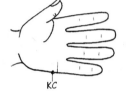

KC

> Even though I am afraid that my parents will get divorced, I am a good kid.
> Even though I am really scared, I am an awesome person.
> Even though I am afraid, I am a good person.

3. Negative Taps
Tap down the points as you say the following:

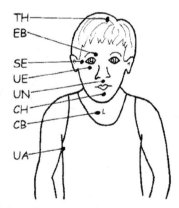

> EB: Divorce is scary.
> SE: My life will change.
> UE: I might have to move.
> UN: I won't see both of my parents all the time.
> CH: I am afraid of divorce.
> CB: It is scary. I do not have any control. No one cares what I think.
> UA: I feel sad. What if I can't live with my brother/sister anymore?
> TH: All of the left over fear and sadness.

Stop tapping.

Take in a super big breath and then blow out all of the air.

4. Forgiving

Hold your hand over your heart as you say the following:

I forgive myself for being afraid; I am doing my best.

I forgive my parents for not getting along; they are doing their best too.

Take in another super big breath and then blow out all of the air.

5. Positive Taps

Tap down the points as you say the following:

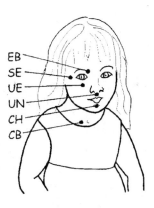

EB: I am safe no matter what happens.

SE: I can let this fear go.

UE: My parents love me.

UN: I am free from this fear.

CH: I can let the fear go.

CB: I am free and safe. Everything will work out for the best.

6. Rate the Intensity

Select on a scale of 0 to 10 how afraid you are that your parents will get divorced, with 10 being the most intense and 0 being not at all.

0	1	2	3	4	5	6	7	8	9	10

Homework

Repeat this process until you feel better.

Problems with Brother or Sister

1. Rate the Intensity

Select on a scale of 0 to 10 how much the problem with your brother or sister bothers you, with 10 being the most intense and 0 being not at all.

0	1	2	3	4	5	6	7	8	9	10

2. Set up

Keep tapping the karate chop point the whole time as you say the following:

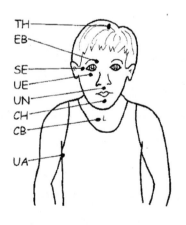

KC

    Even though I am having problems with _____,
I am a good person.
Even though my brother/sister and I do not agree, I am an awesome kid.
Even though I am not getting along with _____, I am the best.

3. Negative Taps

Tap down the points as you say the following:

    EB: We cannot get along.
SE: We never agree.
UE: We always compete.
UN: _____ thinks he/she knows everything.
CH: I am angry.
CB: I know I am right. They blame me for everything.
UA: _____ annoys me.
TH: All of the left over sadness and bad feelings.

Stop tapping.

Take in a super big breath and then blow out all of the air.

4. Forgiving

Hold your hand over your heart as you say the following:

I forgive myself for not getting along with _____; I am doing my best.
I forgive _____ for not getting along with me; he/she is doing the best
that he/she can.

Take in another super big breath and then blow out all of the
air.

5. Positive Taps

Tap down the points as you say the
following:

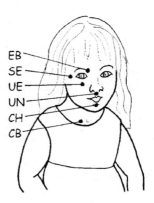

EB: I am letting go of all the bad feelings.
SE: I know we can get along.
UE: Letting go of anything that annoys me.
UN: We can learn to compromise.
CH: Letting all of the anger go, now and
forever.
CB: Feeling happy. Feeling joy.

6. Rate the Intensity

Select on a scale of 0 to 10 how much the problem with your
brother or sister bothers you, with 10 being the most intense
and 0 being not at all.

0	1	2	3	4	5	6	7	8	9	10

Homework

Repeat this process until you know you can work things out with your brother or
sister. You may also choose to work on the "Anger," "Being Made Fun of,"
"Sadness," and "Frustrated" segments of this book.

CHAPTER 4

FEARS

Fears are resolved very easily using EFT. It does not matter whether a fear is real or imagined. It does not matter how irrational a fear may seem. It will have the same affect on the body. There is nothing more liberating for a child than to be free from fear. The segments presented in this chapter will cover common fears that many children experience at some point in their life.

At a very minimum, you should be able to help your child reduce the intensity of the fear so that it is not immobilizing. In many cases there are underlying issues that need to be addressed. If the fear does not completely resolve after working on the segment for several days, ask your child the following questions:

Why do you think you have the fear?

What does this fear remind you of?

What is the first time you remember having this fear?

If you had to guess, what would you think caused the fear?

Once you have the answers to these questions, you can look for other segments in this book to address the underlying causes. Trust your intuition and work on any segment that you think your child will benefit from. There is no harm in overdoing EFT.

Fears

Segments Presented in This Chapter

Fear of:
Animals
The Ball
Clowns
Crowded Places
The Dark
Enclosed Places
Getting Lost
Going to the Dentist
Going to the Doctor
High Places
Monsters/Creatures
Performing/Stage Fright
Roller Coasters and Rides
Spiders
Stormy Weather
Television Show Scared Me
Water/Swimming

Afraid of Animals

1. Rate the Intensity
Select on a scale of 0 to 10 how much animals scare you, with 10 being the most intense and 0 being not at all.

0	1	2	3	4	5	6	7	8	9	10

2. Set up
Keep tapping the karate chop point the whole time as you say the following:

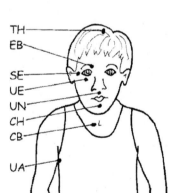

> Even though I am afraid of animals, I am good.
> Even though animals have big scary teeth, I am an awesome kid!
> Even though I have a bad memory about an animal, I can feel safe now.

3. Negative Taps
Tap down the points as you say the following:

> EB: I am scared.
> SE: Animals are mean.
> UE: They want to hurt me.
> UN: They have great big teeth and make scary noises.
> CH: I am afraid. Animals do not listen.
> CB: I do not feel safe.
> UA: I want to hide from animals.
> TH: All of the fear of animals that is left over.

Stop tapping.
Take in a super big breath and then blow out all of the air.

4. Forgiving
Hold your hand over your heart as you say the following:

I forgive myself for being afraid of animals; I am doing my best.
I forgive animals for being scary; they are doing their best, too.

Take in another super big breath and then blow out all of the air.

5. Positive Taps
Tap down the points as you say the following:

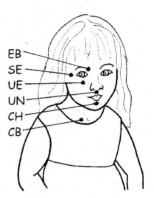

EB: I am not afraid anymore.
SE: I can let go of the fear.
UE: I can feel safe and in control.
UN: I am free of this fear.
CH: I am safe.
CB: I am brave.

6. Rate the Intensity
Select on a scale of 0 to 10 how much animals scare you, with 10 being the most intense and 0 being not at all.

0	1	2	3	4	5	6	7	8	9	10

Homework
Repeat this process everyday for three weeks so that you train your energy not to be afraid. If a certain animal scares you, think about that animal while you are tapping. Remember that not all animals are safe to be around. Make sure you know which animals are friendly and get permission before you go near them.

Afraid of the Ball

1. Rate the Intensity
Select on a scale of 0 to 10 how much the ball scares you, with 10 being the most intense and 0 being not at all.

0	1	2	3	4	5	6	7	8	9	10

2. Set up
Keep tapping the karate chop point the whole time as you say the following:

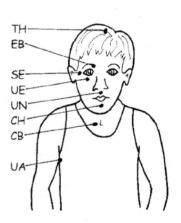

> Even though I am afraid of the ball,
> I am a good person.
> Even though getting hit by a ball hurts, I am an awesome person!
> Even though I do not like playing because I am afraid I will get hit,
> I am a good sport.
> Even though I have a bad memory about being hit by a ball, I can let myself feel safe now.

3. Negative Taps
Tap down the points as you say the following:

> EB: I am scared.
> SE: The ball comes toward me very quickly.
> UE: I am scared because it is fast and hard.
> UN: The ball can hurt me.
> CH: I am afraid. I feel frozen and tense.
> CB: I do not feel safe.
> UA: I want to hide from the ball.
> TH: All of the fear that is left over.

Stop tapping.
Take in a super big breath and then blow out all of the air.

4. Forgiving
Hold your hand over your heart as you say the following:

I forgive myself for being afraid of the ball; I am doing my best.

Take in another super big breath and then blow out all of the air.

5. Positive Taps
Tap down the points as you say the following:

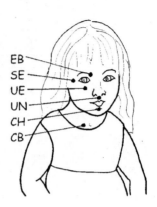

EB: I can let go of the fear.
SE: I am not afraid anymore.
UE: I can feel safe and in control.
UN: I am free of this fear.
CH: I am safe and protected.
CB: I am brave, and I know I can protect myself.

6. Rate the Intensity
Select on a scale of 0 to 10 how much the ball scares you, with 10 being the most intense and 0 being not at all.

0	1	2	3	4	5	6	7	8	9	10

Homework
Repeat this process everyday for three weeks so that you train your energy not to be afraid.

Clowns

1. Rate the Intensity

Select on a scale of 0 to 10 how much clowns scare you, with 10 being the most intense and 0 being not at all.

0	1	2	3	4	5	6	7	8	9	10

2. Set up

Keep tapping the karate chop point the whole time as you say the following:

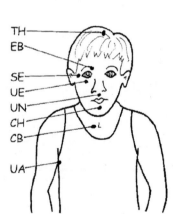

KC

> Even though I am afraid of clowns,
> I chose to let go of the fear.
> Even though clowns are very scary, I am a good boy/girl.
> Even though I am scared just thinking of a clown, I am a great person.

3. Negative Taps

Tap down the points as you say the following:

> EB: Clowns are scary.
> SE: Their faces scare me.
> UE: I am so afraid.
> UN: I do not like to look at them.
> CH: I am afraid to be around them.
> CB: They look scary. They will hurt me.
> UA: I do not trust them.
> TH: All of the left over fear of clowns.

Stop tapping.

Take in a super big breath and then blow out all of the air.

4. Forgiving
Hold your hand over your heart as you say the following:

I forgive myself for being afraid of clowns; I am doing the best I know how.
I forgive clowns for being so scary; they do not mean to scare me.

Take in another super big breath and then blow out all of the air.

5. Positive Taps
Tap down the points as you say the following:

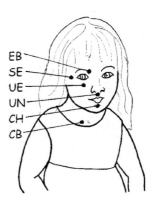

EB: I am letting go of the fear.
SE: Clowns can be funny.
UE: I do feel safe.
UN: I am safe.
CH: I am free from this fear.
CB: This fear is gone forever.

6. Rate the Intensity
Select on a scale of 0 to 10 how much clowns scare you, with 10 being the most intense and 0 being not at all.

0	1	2	3	4	5	6	7	8	9	10

Homework
Close your eyes and picture a scary clown. Think about how you feel. Repeat this process every day until you are no longer afraid when you picture the clown.

Crowded Places

1. Rate the Intensity

Select on a scale of 0 to 10 how much crowded places bother you, with 10 being the most intense and 0 being not at all.

0	1	2	3	4	5	6	7	8	9	10

2. Set up

Keep tapping the karate chop point the whole time as you say the following:

Even though I am afraid in crowded places,
I am a great person.
Even though I do not like being in crowds, I am an awesome kid.
Even though I do not feel good in crowded places, I am completely perfect the way I am.

3. Negative Taps

Tap down the points as you say the following:

EB: It is crowded.
SE: I feel lost.
UE: I do not feel safe.
UN: What if I lose Mom or Dad?
CH: There are so many people.
CB: There is so much action. It is so noisy.
UA: It is scary and I do not feel safe in crowds.
TH: All of the left over bad feelings I have in a crowded place.

Stop tapping.

Take in a super big breath and then blow out all of the air.

4. Forgiving
Hold your hand over your heart as you say the following:

I forgive myself for not liking crowded places; I am doing the best I can.
I forgive all the people for being in those crowded places; they are doing their best and have the right to be there, too.
I forgive my family for taking me to crowded places; they are doing their best.

Take in another super big breath and then blow out all of the air.

5. Positive Taps
Tap down the points as you say the following:

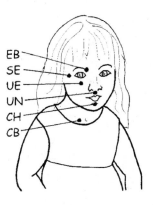

EB: I am letting go of this feeling.
SE: I can release it forever.
UE: It is OK to let go of this fear.
UN: I am safe.
CH: I do feel better. I am tapping into joy.
CB: I can do it!

6. Rate the Intensity
Select on a scale of 0 to 10 how much the thought of being in a crowded place bothers you, with 10 being the most intense and 0 being not at all.

0	1	2	3	4	5	6	7	8	9	10

Homework
Use this process before going to a crowded place. Repeat this until you feel safe and comfortable about going to crowded places.

Afraid of the Dark

1. Rate the Intensity
Select on a scale of 0 to 10 how much the dark scares you, with 10 being the most intense and 0 being not at all.

0	1	2	3	4	5	6	7	8	9	10

2. Set up
Keep tapping the karate chop point the whole time as you say the following:

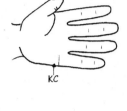

> Even though I am afraid of the dark,
> I am an awesome kid!
> Even though I feel really scared, I can let the fear go.
> Even though I do not feel safe, I chose to be brave.

3. Negative Taps
Tap down the points as you say the following:

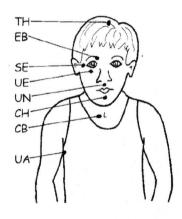

> EB: I am scared.
> SE: Feeling worried.
> UE: Not feeling safe.
> UN: It is dark.
> CH: Not knowing what is around me.
> CB: Not knowing who is around me.
> UA: It is dark and I am afraid when I cannot see.
> TH: Any fear that is left.

Stop tapping.

Take in a super big breath and then blow out all of the air.

4. Forgiving

Hold your hand over your heart as you say the following:

I forgive myself for being afraid of the dark; I am doing my best.
I forgive the darkness for being scary; it is safe and calm.

Take in another super big breath and then blow out all of the air.

5. Positive Taps

Tap down the points as you say the following:

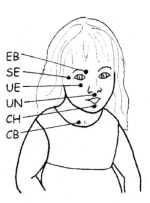

EB: I am safe in the dark.
SE: I can let go of the fear.
UE: I do not have to be afraid anymore.
UN: I am safe. It is peaceful and quiet.
CH: I am comfortable.
CB: I am brave.

6. Rate the Intensity

Select on a scale of 0 to 10 how much the dark scares you, with 10 being the most intense and 0 being not at all.

0	1	2	3	4	5	6	7	8	9	10

Homework

Close your eyes. See and feel the darkness of having your eyes closed. Feel a warm and safe feeling all over. Take a deep breath and then blow it all out. Open your eyes.

Enclosed Places

1. Rate the Intensity
Select on a scale of 0 to 10 how much it bothers you to be in an enclosed place, with 10 being the most intense and 0 being not at all.

0	1	2	3	4	5	6	7	8	9	10

2. Set up
Keep tapping the karate chop point the whole time as you say the following:

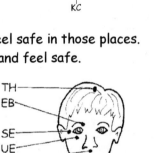

> Even though I am scared to be in
> a closed in place, I am perfect.
> Even though I do not like feeling closed in, I can feel safe in those places.
> Even though I feel afraid, I know I can calm down and feel safe.

3. Negative Taps
Tap down the points as you say the following:

> EB: I am afraid.
> SE: It is scary!
> UE: Everything feels like it is closing in.
> UN: It feels hard to breathe.
> CH: My heart feels heavy.
> CB: I remember a bad time when I felt closed in.
> UA: I do not feel safe when I am in a closed in place.
> TH: All of the left over fear of feeling closed in.

Stop tapping.
Take in a super big breath and then blow out all of the air.

4. Forgiving
Hold your hand over your heart as you say the following:

I forgive myself for being afraid; I am doing my best.
I forgive places that seem scary; they do not mean to scare me.

Take in another super big breath and then blow out all of the air.

5. Positive Taps
Tap down the points as you say the following:

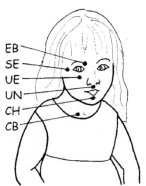

EB: I am safe.
SE: It is OK to let the fear go.
UE: I am happy.
UN: I am a great kid.
CH: I feel safe.
CB: I feel calm and safe. I am tapping in the joy.

6. Rate the Intensity
Select on a scale of 0 to 10 how much it bothers you to think about being in an enclosed place, with 10 being the most intense and 0 being not at all.

0	1	2	3	4	5	6	7	8	9	10

Homework
Close your eyes and imagine you are in a closed-in place such as an elevator or closet. Picture yourself feeling safe, warm, and cozy.

Getting Lost

1. Rate the Intensity
Select on a scale of 0 to 10 how much a bad memory or thinking about getting lost bothers you, with 10 being the most intense and 0 being not at all.

0	1	2	3	4	5	6	7	8	9	10

2. Set up
Keep tapping the karate chop point the whole time as you say the following:

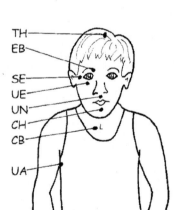

Even though I am afraid of getting lost, I am a good kid.
Even though I remember a very scary time when I got lost, I am awesome.
Even though I cannot stop thinking about getting lost, I am completely perfect how I am.

3. Negative Taps
Tap down the points as you say the following:

EB: I am afraid.
SE: When you are lost, you cannot find anyone you know and trust.
UE: What if I get lost?
UN: What if nobody ever finds me?
CH: What if I can never be with my family again?
CB: I just wouldn't know what to do.
UA: It makes me worry.
TH: All of the left over fear of getting lost.

Stop tapping.
Take in a super big breath and then blow out all of the air.

4. Forgiving
Hold your hand over your heart as you say the following:

I forgive myself for being so afraid of getting lost; I am doing the best I can.

I forgive anyone who may have lost me in the past; they are doing their best and won't let it happen again.

Take in another super big breath and then blow out all of the air.

5. Positive Taps
Tap down the points as you say the following:

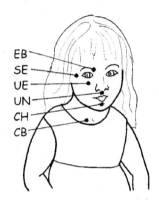

EB: I am safe.
SE: I am protected.
UE: I am letting go of this fear.
UN: I am free of this fear of getting lost.
CH: I am no longer afraid.
CB: I am safe and protected.

6. Rate the Intensity
Select on a scale of 0 to 10 how much thinking about getting lost bothers you, with 10 being the most intense and 0 being not at all.

0	1	2	3	4	5	6	7	8	9	10

Homework
Repeat this process every day until you are free from the fear of getting lost. Remember to always follow your parent's rules for staying together. If you do not know what these rules are, ask your parents. These rules will protect you from getting lost.

Going to the Dentist

1. Rate the Intensity

Select on a scale of 0 to 10 how much going to the dentist bothers you, with 10 being the most intense and 0 being not at all.

| 0 | 1 | 2 | 3 | 4 | 5 | 6 | 7 | 8 | 9 | 10 |

2. Set up

Keep tapping the karate chop point the whole time as you say the following:

Even though I am afraid of going to the dentist, I am perfect the way I am.
Even though I am scared of the noises at the dentist's office, I am brave.
Even though I am afraid it will hurt, I am an awesome patient.

3. Negative Taps

Tap down the points as you say the following:

EB: It is scary.
SE: I am afraid it will hurt. It might make me bleed.
UE: I do not like the noises and smells.
UN: The dentist doesn't seem nice, and I am afraid of him/her.
CH: I do not want to open my mouth. I feel embarrassed.
CB: I do not want to get a shot.
UA: If I have a cavity, it means I am bad at taking care of myself.
TH: All of the left over fear of going to the dentist.

Stop tapping.

Take in a super big breath and then blow out all of the air.

4. Forgiving
Hold your hand over your heart as you say the following:

I forgive myself for being afraid of going to the dentist; I am doing my best. I forgive the dentist for making me scared; the dentist is doing his/her very best to take care of my teeth without hurting me.

Take in another super big breath and then blow out all of the air.

5. Positive Taps
Tap down the points as you say the following:

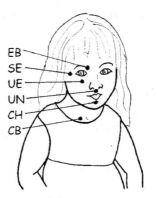

EB: I am brave.
SE: I am safe.
UE: I know that I can handle it. I know it is important to take care of my teeth.
UN: It won't be so bad after all.
CH: I am letting go of all of the left over fear.
CB: I am free from this fear of the dentist.

6. Rate the Intensity
Select on a scale of 0 to 10 how much the thought of going to the dentist bothers you, with 10 being the most intense and 0 being not at all.

0	1	2	3	4	5	6	7	8	9	10

Homework

Repeat this process a few times per day before going to the dentist. If your intensity rating is not down to a zero or a one before your appointment, repeat this several times before seeing the dentist. You can even do it in the car on your way to the dentist's office, and in the waiting area.

Going to the Doctor

1. Rate the Intensity
Select on a scale of 0 to 10 how much going to the doctor bothers you, with 10 being the most intense and 0 being not at all.

0	1	2	3	4	5	6	7	8	9	10

2. Set up
Keep tapping the karate chop point the whole time as you say the following:

KC

> Even though I do not like going to the doctor, I am good.
> Even though I am afraid to go to the doctor, I am an awesome person.
> Even though the doctor's office is cold, I am safe.

3. Negative Taps
Tap down the points as you say the following:

> EB: I am scared.
> SE: I am afraid.
> UE: I do not want to go.
> UN: I am worried. I might get sick.
> CH: It is cold and scary. It smells bad.
> CB: I do not want them to touch me.
> UA: I am afraid the doctor or nurse will hurt me.
> TH: All of the left over fear of going to the doctor.

Stop tapping.
Take in a super big breath and then blow out all of the air.

4. Forgiving
Hold your hand over your heart as you say the following:

     I forgive myself for being afraid to go to the doctor; I am doing my best.
     I forgive the doctor and nurses; they are trying their best to help me.
     I forgive my parents for making me go; they are doing the best they know how.

Take in another super big breath and then blow out all of the air.

5. Positive Taps
Tap down the points as you say the following:

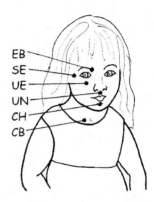

     EB: I am letting go of this fear.
     SE: I can let it go.
     UE: It is not so bad.
     UN: I am strong.
     CH: I am brave.
     CB: I can do it!

6. Rate the Intensity
Select on a scale of 0 to 10 how much the thought of going to the doctor bothers you, with 10 being the most intense and 0 being not at all.

0	1	2	3	4	5	6	7	8	9	10

Homework
Repeat this process several times before you go to the doctor.

Note to parents: This process has been developed for routine doctor's office visits. If your child has a serious illness that requires invasive procedures, please take them to a qualified EFT practitioner for clearing deeper traumas.

High Places

1. Rate the Intensity

Select on a scale of 0 to 10 how much being in a high place bothers you, with 10 being the most intense and 0 being not at all.

0	1	2	3	4	5	6	7	8	9	10

2. Set up

Keep tapping the karate chop point the whole time as you say the following:

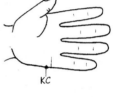

KC

> Even though I am scared of high places, I am an awesome kid.
> Even though I get really nervous when I am up high, I am a great person.
> Even though I have a bad memory of being up high, I am perfect how I am.

3. Negative Taps

Tap down the points as you say the following:

> EB: I am scared.
> SE: I do not like to look down.
> UE: It makes me nervous to think about how up high I am.
> UN: I do not feel safe. My legs feel weak.
> CH: I am not safe.
> CB: I am not in control. My body feels unable to move.
> UA: I could fall and get hurt.
> TH: All of the left over fear of high places.

Stop tapping.

Take in a super big breath and then blow out all of the air.

4. Forgiving
Hold your hand over your heart as you say the following:

I forgive myself for being afraid of high places; I am doing the best I know how.

I forgive myself for feeling so scared; I am doing my best.

Take in another super big breath and then blow out all of the air.

5. Positive Taps
Tap down the points as you say the following:

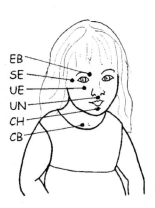

EB: I am letting go of this fear.

SE: I can safely be up high without feeling bad.

UE: Letting go of all of the fear.

UN: Feeling safe and secure.

CH: Feeling protected. I am tapping in the joy.

CB: Feeling in control.

6. Rate the Intensity
Select on a scale of 0 to 10 how much being in a high place bothers you, with 10 being the most intense and 0 being not at all.

0	1	2	3	4	5	6	7	8	9	10

Homework
Close your eyes and imagine you are up high on a ladder. Think about how that would make you feel. If you still feel scared, repeat the process every day until you can imagine yourself in a high place without feeling uncomfortable.

Monsters/Creatures

1. Rate the Intensity
Select on a scale of 0 to 10 how much monsters/creatures bother you, with 10 being the most intense and 0 being not at all.

0	1	2	3	4	5	6	7	8	9	10

2. Set up
Keep tapping the karate chop point the whole time as you say the following:

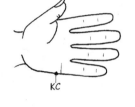

KC

> Even though I am afraid of monsters,
> I am an awesome kid.
> Even though monsters are scary, I am a good boy/girl.
> Even though I believe monsters are hiding in my room, I choose not to be afraid.

3. Negative Taps
Tap down the points as you say the following:

> EB: I am afraid of monsters.
> SE: I am afraid of creepy things.
> UE: It is not easy.
> UN: They are bad creatures.
> What if they are real?
> CH: Monsters are scary. They are big and strong. They might hurt me.
> CB: Monsters might be hiding in my closet or under the bed.
> UA: They will come out and get me. They will get my family.
> TH: All of the left over fear and worry.

Stop tapping.
Take in a super big breath and then blow out all of the air.

4. Forgiving

Hold your hand over your heart as you say the following:

> I forgive myself for being afraid of monsters; I am doing my best.
> I forgive monsters for being in my imagination; everything will be OK.

Take in another super big breath and then blow out all of the air.

5. Positive Taps

Tap down the points as you say the following:

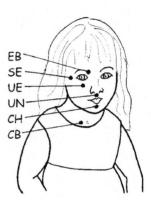

> EB: I am brave.
> SE: I know monsters aren't real.
> UE: Letting all of the fear go.
> UN: Feeling safe and happy.
> CH: Feeling free of this fear.
> CB: Not afraid anymore.

6. Rate the Intensity

Select on a scale of 0 to 10 how much monsters/creatures bother you, with 10 being the most intense and 0 being not at all.

0	1	2	3	4	5	6	7	8	9	10

Homework

Repeat this process until you are no longer afraid of monsters.

Note to parents: Fears can be caused by actual events or can be imagined, but to the young mind, it doesn't matter. You can substitute any specific creature for "monsters" simply by filling in the appropriate word in the dialogue above.

Performing/Stage Fright

1. Rate the Intensity
Select on a scale of 0 to 10 how much your stage fright bothers you, with 10 being the most intense and 0 being not at all.

0	1	2	3	4	5	6	7	8	9	10

2. Set up
Keep tapping the karate chop point the whole time as you say the following:

> Even though I am afraid of performing in front of people, I am a good person.
> Even though I have stage fright, I am an awesome kid.
> Even though I do not feel safe and comfortable, I am a good student.

3. Negative Taps
Tap down the points as you say the following:

> EB: I am afraid of being in front of an audience.
> SE: I do not like reading my report/giving a presentation/performing on stage.
> UE: I feel nervous.
> UN: My whole body feels like it is trembling inside.
> CH: Everyone is looking at me. They are listening to everything I say. What if they make fun of me?
> CB: What if I make a mistake? I will be embarrassed.
> UA: I cannot do it.
> TH: All of the left over stage fright.

Stop tapping.
Take in a super big breath and then blow out all of the air.

4. Forgiving
Hold your hand over your heart as you say the following:

I forgive myself for having stage fright; I am doing the best I know how.

I forgive the audience for staring at me; they are doing the best they can.

Take in another super big breath and then blow out all of the air.

5. Positive Taps
Tap down the points as you say the following:

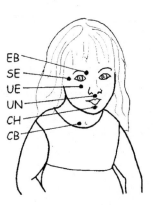

EB: I am letting go of the fear.

SE: I can be free of this fear.

UE: I am not nervous. I am thinking clearly.

UN: I feel confident. My words and actions show my confidence.

CH: I am comfortable.

CB: I can do this.

6. Rate the Intensity
Select on a scale of 0 to 10 how much your stage fright bothers you, with 10 being the most intense and 0 being not at all.

0	1	2	3	4	5	6	7	8	9	10

Homework
Repeat this process two or three times per day for two days before your presentation/performance.

Roller Coasters and Rides

1. Rate the Intensity
Select on a scale of 0 to 10 how afraid you are of going on rides, with 10 being the most intense and 0 being not at all.

0	1	2	3	4	5	6	7	8	9	10

2. Set up
Keep tapping the karate chop point the whole time as you say the following:

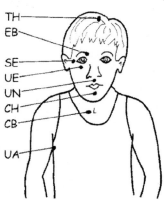

KC

> Even though I am scared of riding on roller coasters, I am awesome.
> Even though roller coasters are fast, I am an awesome person.
> Even though roller coasters are high up and I do not feel safe, I am a good person.

3. Negative Taps
Tap down the points as you say the following:

> EB: I am really scared.
> SE: It might break and I will get hurt.
> UE: It is really fast. It makes me feel sick.
> UN: Once it starts, you cannot get off.
> CH: Waiting in line makes me feel scared.
> CB: Hearing other kids scream makes me afraid.
> UA: I cannot take it. I cannot do it. I do not trust those rides.
> TH: All of the left over fear about riding on roller coasters.

Stop tapping.
Take in a super big breath and then blow out all of the air.

4. Forgiving

Hold your hand over your heart as you say the following:

I forgive myself for being afraid; I am doing the best I know how.
I forgive other people for wanting me to go on the roller coaster;
they do not understand how bad it makes me feel.

Take in another super big breath and then blow out all of the air.

5. Positive Taps

Tap down the points as you say the following:

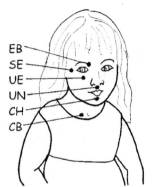

EB: I am letting the fear go away.
SE: I can let it go.
UE: I can trust that the ride is safe.
UN: I can have fun just like the other kids.
CH: I am brave.
CB: I can relax and let myself safely enjoy the ride.

6. Rate the Intensity

Select on a scale of 0 to 10 how afraid you are of going on rides, with 10 being the most intense and 0 being not at all.

0	1	2	3	4	5	6	7	8	9	10

Homework

Begin working on this process one or two days before going to a carnival or amusement park where you will be able to go on rides. Repeat the process five or six times before you go. Imagine you are there and see how you feel. You might also want to work on the "High Places" segment of this book.

Spiders

1. Rate the Intensity
Select on a scale of 0 to 10 how afraid you are of spiders, with 10 being the most intense and 0 being not at all.

0	1	2	3	4	5	6	7	8	9	10

2. Set up
Keep tapping the karate chop point the whole time as you say the following:

KC

Even though I do not like spiders,
I am an awesome kid.
Even though I am really afraid of spiders,
I know I will be able to get over this.
Even though I do not like seeing spiders, I am a good person.

3. Negative Taps
Tap down the points as you say the following:

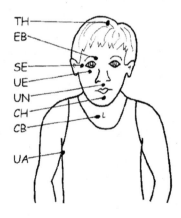

EB: Spiders are scary.
SE: They look freaky.
UE: They want to crawl on me and bite me.
UN: I see other people who are afraid of spiders too.
CH: I do not like spiders.
CB: I am really afraid.
UA: Spiders are sneaky and creepy.
TH: All of the left over fear of spiders.

Stop tapping.
Take in a super big breath and then blow out all of the air.

4. Forgiving

Hold your hand over your heart as you say the following:

> I forgive myself for being afraid of spiders; I am doing my best.
> I forgive spiders for looking scary and mean; they are just being spiders!

Take in another super big breath and then blow out all of the air.

5. Positive Taps

Tap down the points as you say the following:

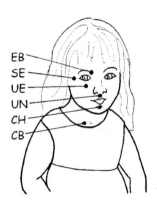

> EB: I am letting go of this fear.
> SE: I can let go of any bad memories about spiders.
> UE: I am free from this fear.
> UN: I am safe and secure.
> CH: Spiders aren't so bad after all.
> CB: I am comfortable and free.

6. Rate the Intensity

Select on a scale of 0 to 10 how afraid you are of spiders, with 10 being the most intense and 0 being not at all.

0	1	2	3	4	5	6	7	8	9	10

Homework

Repeat this process until you no longer feel afraid of spiders.
You can substitute bees, mosquitos, other insects, or snakes in place of spiders.

Stormy Weather

1. Rate the Intensity
Select on a scale of 0 to 10 how afraid you are of stormy weather, with 10 being the most intense and 0 being not at all.

0	1	2	3	4	5	6	7	8	9	10

2. Set up
Keep tapping the karate chop point the whole time as you say the following:

> Even though I am afraid of storms,
> I completely accept myself.
> Even though storms really scare me, I am a good person.
> Even though I do not feel safe when it is storming, I am an awesome kid.

3. Negative Taps
Tap down the points as you say the following:

> EB: Storms are scary.
> SE: Storms are dangerous.
> UE: Thunder and lightning are loud and can hurt me.
> UN: I do not feel safe. I am not protected.
> CH: What if a tornado comes?
> CB: I cannot relax. I am so tense.
> UA: I am afraid of getting hurt. I am afraid someone I love will get hurt.
> TH: All of the left over fear of storms.

Stop tapping.

Take in a super big breath and then blow out all of the air.

4. Forgiving
Hold your hand over your heart as you say the following:

I forgive myself for being afraid; I am doing the best I know how.
I forgive weather for being so scary; it is all part of nature.

Take in another super big breath and then blow out all of the air.

5. Positive Taps
Tap down the points as you say the following:

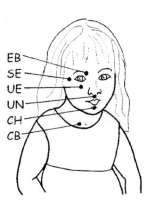

EB: I am letting go of all of the fear.
SE: I can release it forever.
UE: I am free from this fear.
UN: I am protected.
CH: I will be OK. I can be brave even if someone else is scared
CB: I am safe and secure.

6. Rate the Intensity
Select on a scale of 0 to 10 how scared you are of stormy weather, with 10 being the most intense and 0 being not at all.

0	1	2	3	4	5	6	7	8	9	10

Homework
Repeat this process anytime it is storming until you no longer feel afraid.

Television Show Scared Me

1. Rate the Intensity
Select on a scale of 0 to 10 how much the television show scared you, with 10 being the most intense and 0 being not at all.

0	1	2	3	4	5	6	7	8	9	10

2. Set up
Keep tapping the karate chop point the whole time as you say the following:

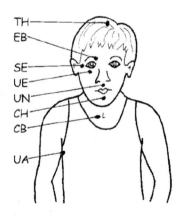

KC

Even though I am afraid of what I saw on TV,
I choose to let go of the fear.
Even though there are scary things on TV, I am a good person.
Even though I am scared just thinking about it, I am a great person.

3. Negative Taps
Tap down the points as you say the following:

EB: TV scared me.
SE: What I saw scared me.
UE: I am so afraid.
UN: I do not like to think about it.
I cannot stop thinking about it.
CH: I am afraid. What if it is real?
What if it hurts me/happens to me?
CB: I wasn't supposed to see that.
UA: That scary show is real.
TH: All of the left over fear.

Stop tapping.
Take in a super big breath and then blow out all of the air.

4. Forgiving
Hold your hand over your heart as you say the following:

I forgive myself for being afraid; I am doing the best I know how.
I forgive myself for seeing it; I didn't know it was going to scare me.

Take in another super big breath and then blow out all of the air.

5. Positive Taps
Tap down the points as you say the following:

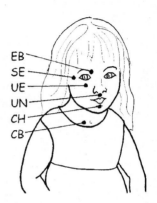

EB: I am letting go of the fear.
SE: I can get rid of that thought.
UE: I do feel safe.
UN: I am safe now.
CH: I am free from that thought.
CB: This fear is gone forever.

6. Rate the Intensity
Select on a scale of 0 to 10 how much the television show scared you, with 10 being the most intense and 0 being not at all.

0	1	2	3	4	5	6	7	8	9	10

Homework
Repeat this process every day until you are no longer afraid of what you saw.

Note to parents: Unfortunately, kids of all ages catch a glimpse of something scary on TV. Images and stories on the news really frighten children. If they are watching a lot of TV, they should do this segment regularly because they are undoubtedly seeing some scary images.

Water/Swimming

1. Rate the Intensity
Select on a scale of 0 to 10 how scared you are of the water, with 10 being the most intense and 0 being not at all.

0	1	2	3	4	5	6	7	8	9	10

2. Set up
Keep tapping the karate chop point the whole time as you say the following:

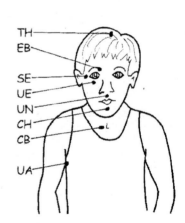

> Even though I am afraid of water, I am awesome.
> Even though water scares me, I am a good person.
> Even though I have a bad memory about water, I totally accept myself.

3. Negative Taps
Tap down the points as you say the following:

> EB: I am afraid of water.
> SE: I do not like it.
> UE: It is cold. It is wet. It is smelly.
> It burns my eyes.
> UN: I cannot go into the water.
> CH: I cannot swim. I will never learn.
> CB: My body doesn't cooperate.
> UA: I cannot put my face in the water.
> TH: All of the left over fear of the water.

Stop tapping.
Take in a super big breath and then blow out all of the air.

4. Forgiving

Hold your hand over your heart as you say the following:

> I forgive myself for being afraid of the water; I am doing the best I know how.
>
> I forgive myself for not being able to swim; I am doing my best.

Take in another super big breath and then blow out all of the air.

5. Positive Taps

Tap down the points as you say the following:

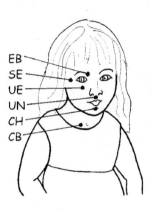

> EB: I am letting go of this fear.
> SE: I can let it go forever.
> UE: I can learn to swim.
> UN: I can do it safely. I will follow all the rules.
> CH: My body is cooperating, and I can learn to swim.
> CB: It is easy. I can do it.

6. Rate the Intensity

Select on a scale of 0 to 10 how scared you are of the water, with 10 being the most intense and 0 being not at all.

0	1	2	3	4	5	6	7	8	9	10

Homework

Warning: It is very important that you never go near water unless a grown up is watching you and has given you permission. Note to parents: This process is intended to help children feel safe about getting in the water to take swim lessons. This is one of those processes where you do not want to haphazardly remove the fear of water. A certain level of fear or respect is appropriate.

CHAPTER 5

SCHOOL

The segments in this chapter relate to school and the problems that your child may be experiencing.

These segments will help your child to conquer fears, achieve focus, and overcome limiting beliefs that are preventing them from working to their potential.

If your child is experiencing fears, or is troubled by the school bus, see Chapter 6—Transportation.

School

Segments Presented in This Chapter

Cannot Learn Math Facts
Do Not Want to Do Homework
First Day of School
Issues with Teacher
Reading Is a Struggle
Test Taking

Cannot Learn Math Facts

1. Rate the Intensity
Select on a scale of 0 to 10 how much it bothers you that you are having a hard time learning your math facts, with 10 being the most intense and 0 being not at all.

0	1	2	3	4	5	6	7	8	9	10

2. Set up
Keep tapping the karate chop point the whole time as you say the following:

KC

> Even though I cannot learn my math facts,
> I am a good student.
> Even though math is hard, I am smart.
> Even though it is hard to remember all of these facts, I am perfect the way I am.

3. Negative Taps
Tap down the points as you say the following:

> EB: I cannot learn these facts.
> SE: Math is too hard.
> It is hard to remember how to do it.
> UE: It is frustrating.
> UN: It is confusing. I cannot remember how to do it.
> CH: My teacher will get mad if I ask a question.
> CB: Other kids are smarter. I am just not smart enough.
> UA: I just do not get it.
> TH: All of the left over feelings that I cannot learn these facts.

Stop tapping.
Take in a super big breath and then blow out all of the air.

4. Forgiving
Hold your hand over your heart as you say the following:

I forgive myself for not learning these facts; I am doing my best.
I forgive myself for not remembering these facts; I am doing the best I know how.

Take in another super big breath and then blow out all of the air.

5. Positive Taps
Tap down the points as you say the following:

Review the appropriate math facts,
while tapping one problem at each point.
For example:

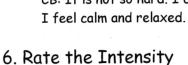

EB: 2+2=4
SE: 2+4=6
UE: 4+2=6
UN: 2+3=5
CH: 3+2=5
CB: It is not so hard. I can remember. I choose to let it be easy. I can do it! I feel calm and relaxed.

6. Rate the Intensity
Select on a scale of 0 to 10 how much it bothers you that it is difficult to learn your math facts, with 10 being the most intense and 0 being not at all.

0	1	2	3	4	5	6	7	8	9	10

Homework
Repeat this process each day using different groups of appropriate math facts.
Note to parents: Focus on small groups until your child has mastered that group, then move to a particular set of facts that your child seems to struggle with.

Do Not Want to Do Homework

1. Rate the Intensity

Select on a scale of 0 to 10 how much it bothers you to think about doing your homework, with 10 being the most intense and 0 being not at all.

0	1	2	3	4	5	6	7	8	9	10

2. Set up

Keep tapping the karate chop point the whole time as you say the following:

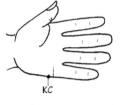

KC

> Even though I do not want to do my homework,
> I am a good student.
> Even though I do not like doing my homework, I am an awesome person.
> Even though it is frustrating when I cannot concentrate, I am a smart person.

3. Negative Taps

Tap down the points as you say the following:

> EB: I do not want to do it.
> SE: I do not have time.
> UE: I cannot figure it out.
> UN: It is hard. I am not smart enough.
> CH: It is frustrating. I cannot sit still.
> CB: I cannot do it. I keep avoiding it.
> UA: I won't do it.
> TH: All of the left over problems with getting my homework done.

Stop tapping.

Take in a super big breath and then blow out all of the air.

4. Forgiving
Hold your hand over your heart as you say the following:

I forgive myself for not wanting to do my homework; I am doing my best.

I forgive myself for not understanding it; I am doing the best I know how.

Take in another super big breath and then blow out all of the air.

5. Positive Taps
Tap down the points as you say the following:

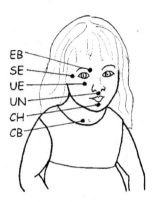

EB: I am capable of doing this.

SE: I can do it. I can try.

I can figure this out.

UE: It is my responsibility.

UN: It will get easier. I am smart.

CH: I can achieve success.

CB: I will succeed.

6. Rate the Intensity
Select on a scale of 0 to 10 how much it bothers you to think about doing your homework, with 10 being the most intense and 0 being not at all.

0	1	2	3	4	5	6	7	8	9	10

Homework
This homework is easy! No studying. No tests. Simply follow the process above until you feel empowered to complete your assignments. You may also want to work on the "Frustrated," "Hard to Pay Attention," and "I Cannot Do It" segments of this book.

First Day of School

1. Rate the Intensity
Select on a scale of 0 to 10 how much the thought of the first day of school bothers you, with 10 being the most intense and 0 being not at all.

0	1	2	3	4	5	6	7	8	9	10

2. Set up
Keep tapping the karate chop point the whole time as you say the following:

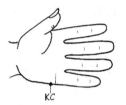

> Even though I am afraid to go to school,
> I am an awesome kid.
> Even though I won't know anybody, I am a good person.
> Even though the school is a big scary place, I love and accept myself.

3. Negative Taps
Tap down the points as you say the following:

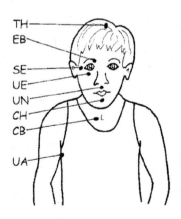

> EB: I am really afraid.
> SE: I do not want to go to school.
> I do not want to grow up.
> UE: What if I do not know anyone?
> No one can stay with me.
> UN: I do not know my way around. It is a big place.
> CH: What if I get lost?
> CB: I am really scared. What if it is not safe?
> UA: It will be really hard.
> TH: All of the left over fear about going to school.

Stop tapping.
Take in a super big breath and then blow out all of the air.

4. Forgiving
Hold your hand over your heart as you say the following:

I forgive myself for being afraid; I am doing the best I know how.

I forgive myself for not wanting to go to school; I am doing my very best.

Take in another super big breath and then blow out all of the air.

5. Positive Taps
Tap down the points as you say the following:

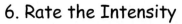

EB: I am going to allow myself to let go of this fear.

SE: I can let it go.

UE: I am feeling free of this fear.

UN: School is fun. The teachers will tell me where to go and what to do.

CH: They will make sure I am safe and that I am where I am supposed to be.

CB: I am safe and happy about going to school.

6. Rate the Intensity
Select on a scale of 0 to 10 how much thinking of the first day of school bothers you, with 10 being the most intense and 0 being not at all.

0	1	2	3	4	5	6	7	8	9	10

Homework
Repeat this a few times every day until you are feeling happy about going to school.

Issues with Teacher

1. Rate the Intensity
Select on a scale of 0 to 10 how much the issue with your teacher bothers you, with 10 being the most intense and 0 being not at all.

0	1	2	3	4	5	6	7	8	9	10

2. Set up
Keep tapping the karate chop point the whole time as you say the following:

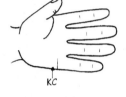

KC

    Even though I think my teacher doesn't like me, I am a good student.
    Even though I am afraid to answer questions, I can believe in myself.
    Even though my teacher thinks I started something, I know the truth.

3. Negative Taps
Tap down the points as you say the following:

    EB: My teacher seems mean.
    She/He doesn't like me.
    SE: I am afraid I will let her/him down if I do not give the right answer.
    UE: I am afraid to ask a question.
    UN: I always get blamed for things I didn't do.
    CH: I do not like getting corrected.
    CB: My teacher hurts my feelings.
    UA: I do not feel safe asking for help. He or she gets mad.
    TH: All of the left over bad feelings about my teacher.

Stop tapping.
Take in a super big breath and then blow out all of the air.

4. Forgiving
Hold your hand over your heart as you say the following:

I forgive myself for feeling this way; I am doing the best I know how.
I forgive my teacher; he/she is doing the best he/she can.

Take in another super big breath and then blow out all of the air.

5. Positive Taps
Tap down the points as you say the following:

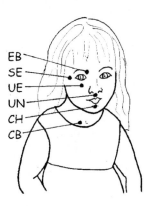

EB: I am letting go of the bad feelings.
SE: My teacher is there to help me.
UE: I am at school to learn.
UN: I am smart.
CH: I feel safe asking questions.
CB: I can ask for help with anything I do not understand.

6. Rate the Intensity
Select on a scale of 0 to 10 how much the issue with your teacher bothers you, with 10 being the most intense and 0 being not at all.

0	1	2	3	4	5	6	7	8	9	10

Homework
Repeat this process a few times every day until you feel good about the situation.

Reading Is a Struggle

1. Rate the Intensity
Select on a scale of 0 to 10 how hard it is for you to read, with 10 being the most intense and 0 being not at all.

0	1	2	3	4	5	6	7	8	9	10

2. Set up
Keep tapping the karate chop point the whole time as you say the following:

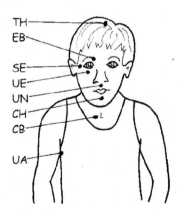

> Even though it is really hard to read and understand what I read, I am an awesome kid.
> Even though I cannot read as good as other kids, I am a good student.
> Even though I am having a hard time, I am able to succeed.

3. Negative Taps
Tap down the points as you say the following:

> EB: Reading is hard. It has always been hard for me.
> SE: It is boring.
> UE: I struggle.
> UN: I cannot do it. It is too hard.
> CH: The words do not make any sense. It is hard to sound them out.
> CB: The story doesn't make any sense.
> UA: I cannot put it all together.
> TH: All of the left over struggle with reading.

Stop tapping.
Take in a super big breath and then blow out all of the air.

4. Forgiving

Hold your hand over your heart as you say the following:

> I forgive myself for not being able to read better; I am doing my best.
> I forgive books for being hard to understand.
> I forgive my parents and teachers for making me read; they are trying to help me to become a better reader.

Take in another super big breath and then blow out all of the air.

5. Positive Taps

Tap down the points as you say the following:

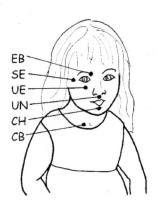

> EB: I am letting go of everything that makes reading so hard for me.
> SE: It is becoming clear to me. It is making sense.
> UE: I understand what I read.
> UN: Reading is exciting.
> CH: Reading is easy.
> CB: It is easy and fun.

6. Rate the Intensity

Select on a scale of 0 to 10 how hard it is for you to read, with 10 being the most intense and 0 being not at all.

0	1	2	3	4	5	6	7	8	9	10

Homework

Repeat this process two or three times per day until you find that reading becomes easier and easier for you.

Test Taking

1. Rate the Intensity
Select on a scale of 0 to 10 how much taking a test bothers you, with 10 being the most intense and 0 being not at all.

0	1	2	3	4	5	6	7	8	9	10

2. Set up
Keep tapping the karate chop point the whole time as you say the following:

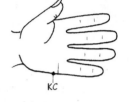

> Even though I do not like taking tests,
> I am a good student.
> Even though I am afraid of taking tests, I am an awesome kid.
> Even though taking a test makes me feel jittery, I know I can get over this.
> Even though I cannot remember the answers when I take a test, I am a good student.

3. Negative Taps
Tap down the points as you say the following:

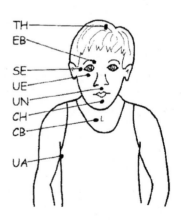

> EB: I worry about taking tests.
> SE: They are really hard.
> UE: I forget the answers.
> UN: I feel like they are trying to trick me.
> CH: I feel anxious.
> CB: I cannot relax and think clearly.
> UA: I feel so much pressure that if I do not do well, I will get a bad grade.
> TH: All of the left over bad feelings about having to take a test.

Stop tapping.
Take in a super big breath and then blow out all of the air.

4. Forgiving

Hold your hand over your heart as you say the following:

I forgive myself for not liking to take tests; I am doing the best I can.
I forgive myself for getting anxious; I am doing the best I know how.

Take in another super big breath and then blow out all of the air.

5. Positive Taps

Tap down the points as you say the following:

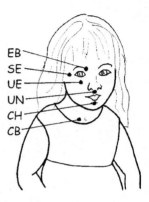

EB: I am letting go of this fear.
SE: I can let go of any anxiety.
UE: I am safe and protected.
UN: I am grateful that I can remain calm while taking tests.
CH: I remember what I have studied.
CB: I follow the directions, and I know what to do.

6. Rate the Intensity

Select on a scale of 0 to 10 how much it bothers you to take a test, with 10 being the most intense and 0 being not at all.

0	1	2	3	4	5	6	7	8	9	10

Homework
Repeat this process daily until you feel comfortable and confident taking tests.

CHAPTER 6

TRANSPORTATION

The segments in this chapter address fears, motion sickness, and limiting beliefs as they relate to modes of transportation.

Transportation

Segments Presented in This Chapter

Airplanes
School Buses
Riding a Bike
Riding in the Car

Airplanes

1. Rate the Intensity
Select on a scale of 0 to 10 how much flying in airplanes scares you, with 10 being the most intense and 0 being not at all.

0	1	2	3	4	5	6	7	8	9	10

2. Set up
Keep tapping the karate chop point the whole time as you say the following:

> Even though I am afraid to be in an airplane, I am a good person.
> Even though I do not feel safe, I am able to let it go.
> Even though I remember bad things about airplanes, I am safe.

3. Negative Taps
Tap down the points as you say the following:

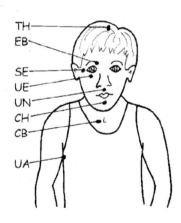

> EB: I feel scared. I feel sick.
> SE: I do not feel safe.
> UE: Airplanes could crash.
> UN: It is scary to take off.
> CH: It is scary to land.
> CB: Other people get scared.
> UA: Letting all of the fear go away.
> TH: All of the fear of airplanes that is left over.

Stop tapping.
Take in a super big breath and then blow out all of the air.

4. Forgiving
Hold your hand over your heart as you say the following:

I forgive myself for being afraid; I am trying my best.
I forgive airplanes for being so big and scary.

Take in another super big breath and then blow out all of the air.

5. Positive Taps
Tap down the points as you say the following:

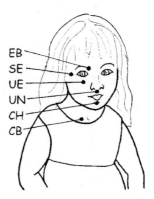

EB: I am safe.
SE: I can feel good and have fun on an airplane.
UE: Lots of smart people are working very hard to keep airplanes safe.
UN: I am free of this fear.
CH: I am free to explore new places.
CB: I am safe and happy.

6. Rate the Intensity
Select on a scale of 0 to 10 how much flying in airplanes scares you, with 10 being the most intense and 0 being not at all.

0	1	2	3	4	5	6	7	8	9	10

Homework
Close your eyes and imagine yourself getting on an airplane. You are going to fly to the best place you can imagine. You feel safe and happy. Take a great big deep breath. Blow it out your mouth as hard as you can. Blowing away anything that scares you. Now pretend that you are getting off the plane and it is better than you ever imagined. Open your eyes. How do you feel?

School Buses

1. Rate the Intensity

Select on a scale of 0 to 10 how much the thought of going on a school bus bothers you, with 10 being the most intense and 0 being not at all.

0	1	2	3	4	5	6	7	8	9	10

2. Set up

Keep tapping the karate chop point the whole time as you say the following:

KC

> Even though I do not like going on the bus,
> I am perfect.
> Even though I am afraid of riding on the bus, I am an awesome person.
> Even though kids might make fun of me on the bus, I am a good person.

3. Negative Taps

Tap down the points as you say the following:

> EB: I do not like riding on the bus.
> SE: The bus is big and scary. What if it does not take me to the right place?
> UE: Kids on the bus are big and scary.
> UN: The bus ride is bumpy and noisy. It stinks on the bus.
> CH: Kids might make fun of me. I feel sick.
> CB: I might have to sit with someone that I do not want to sit with.
> UA: I just want to stay home. I want someone to drive me to school.
> TH: All of the left over fear and bad feelings about riding on the bus.

Stop tapping.

Take in a super big breath and then blow out all of the air.

4. Forgiving
Hold your hand over your heart as you say the following:

I forgive myself for not wanting to ride on the bus; I am doing my best.

I forgive myself for being afraid; I am doing the best I know how.

Take in another super big breath and then blow out all of the air.

5. Positive Taps
Tap down the points as you say the following:

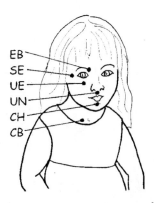

EB: I am letting go of all the bad feelings about the bus.

SE: I can feel safe and have fun on the bus.

UE: Riding the bus is safe.

UN: Letting go of all of the fear. Letting it all go.

CH: I am safe and happy.

CB: I am strong and brave.

6. Rate the Intensity
Select on a scale of 0 to 10 how much the thought of going on a school bus bothers you, with 10 being the most intense and 0 being not at all.

0	1	2	3	4	5	6	7	8	9	10

Homework
Repeat this process every day until you feel good about riding the bus. You may also want to work on the "First Day of School," "Do Not Like to Be Apart or Separated," "Being Bullied," or "Being Made Fun of" segments of this book.

Riding a Bike

1. Rate the Intensity
Select on a scale of 0 to 10 how hard it is for you to ride a bike, with 10 being the most intense and 0 being not at all.

0	1	2	3	4	5	6	7	8	9	10

2. Set up
Keep tapping the karate chop point the whole time as you say the following:

> Even though I cannot ride a bike, I am a good sport.
> Even though I am afraid to ride a bike, I am a an awesome person.
> Even though I am afraid I will fall and get hurt, I am a good kid.

3. Negative Taps
Tap down the points as you say the following:

> EB: Riding a bike is scary.
> SE: Falling down hurts.
> UE: I cannot do it.
> UN: I am not good at it.
> CH: I cannot ride my bike without the training wheels (if appropriate).
> CB: It is too hard.
> UA: I might fall.
> TH: All of the left over fear of riding a bike.

Stop tapping.
Take in a super big breath and then blow out all of the air.

4. Forgiving
Hold your hand over your heart as you say the following:

> I forgive myself for being afraid to ride my bike; I am doing the best I can.
> I forgive my bike for scaring me; it doesn't mean to scare me.

Take in another super big breath and then blow out all of the air.

5. Positive Taps
Tap down the points as you say the following:

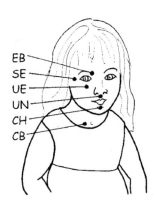

> EB: I am free from this fear.
> SE: I can let it go.
> UE: I can do it.
> UN: I can take my time and ride carefully.
> CH: I know I can do it. I will be OK.
> CB: I can do it just like other kids. I can ride my bike!

6. Rate the Intensity
Select on a scale of 0 to 10 how hard you think it is to ride a bike, with 10 being the most intense and 0 being not at all.

0	1	2	3	4	5	6	7	8	9	10

Homework
Repeat this process until you feel confident that you can ride your bike. You may also wish to work on the "I Cannot Do It" segment of this book.

Riding in the Car

1. Rate the Intensity
Select on a scale of 0 to 10 how much riding in the car bothers you, with 10 being the most intense and 0 being not at all.

0	1	2	3	4	5	6	7	8	9	10

2. Set up
Keep tapping the karate chop point the whole time as you say the following:

KC

> Even though I do not like riding in the car, I am a good person.
> Even though I am afraid to ride in the car, I am a good kid.
> Even though I do not feel good about riding in the car, I am awesome!
> Even though riding in the car makes me feel sick, I am able to feel good about it.

3. Negative Taps
Tap down the points as you say the following:

> EB: I do not like it.
> SE: Cars make me feel bad.
> UE: I feel sick.
> UN: I feel afraid.
> CH: I feel closed in. The air feels bad.
> CB: I am afraid of getting trapped.
> UA: It gives me butterflies in my tummy.
> TH: All of the left over bad feelings about riding in the car.

Stop tapping.

Take in a super big breath and then blow out all of the air.

4. Forgiving

Hold your hand over your heart as you say the following:

> I forgive myself for not liking to ride in the car; I am doing the best I can.
> I forgive the car for making me feel bad.
> I forgive my family for not understanding why I do not like riding in the car;
> they are doing the best they know how.

Take in another super big breath and then blow out all of the air.

5. Positive Taps

Tap down the points as you say the following:

> EB: I am letting go of all the bad feelings.
> SE: I can feel safe.
> UE: I can feel good.
> UN: I do not have to think about the bad things while I am in the car.
> CH: I am safe and comfortable.
> CB: I feel good about going in the car. The car takes me to lots of great places.

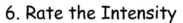

6. Rate the Intensity

Select on a scale of 0 to 10 how much the thought of riding in the car bothers you, with 10 being the most intense and 0 being not at all.

0	1	2	3	4	5	6	7	8	9	10

Homework

Repeat this process until you do feel good about riding in the car.

CHAPTER 7

OTHER EMOTIONS AND ISSUES

The segments in this chapter address a variety of emotions and issues that can be easily overcome using EFT. It is important that you are consistent with working through these issues with your child. You may find that you need to repeat them several times per day. The results will be worth the time that you invest!

Other Emotions and Issues

Segments Presented in This Chapter

Anger
Anxious/Anxiety
Frustrated
Getting Yelled At
Grief – Loss of Loved One
Grief – Loss of Pet
Guilt
Hard to Pay Attention
Impatient
Lost Something Special
Loud Noises
Sadness
Trouble Sleeping

Anger

1. Rate the Intensity

Select on a scale of 0 to 10 how much anger you feel, with 10 being the most intense and 0 being not at all.

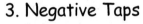

| 0 | 1 | 2 | 3 | 4 | 5 | 6 | 7 | 8 | 9 | 10 |

2. Set up

Keep tapping the karate chop point the whole time as you say the following:

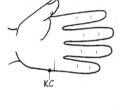

> Even though I am really mad, I am an awesome kid.
> Even though I am angry, I love and accept myself.
> Even though I feel mad, I am a good person.

3. Negative Taps

Tap down the points as you say the following:

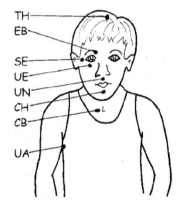

> EB: I am angry.
> SE: I am mad.
> UE: It is not fair.
> UN: I feel tightness inside of me.
> CH: It feels bad.
> CB: Feeling the anger all over my body.
> UA: I am really mad.
> TH: All of the left over anger.

Stop tapping.

Take in a super big breath and then blow out all of the air.

4. Forgiving
Hold your hand over your heart as you say the following:
> I forgive myself for feeling this way; I am doing the best I can.
> I forgive whoever made me mad; they didn't know any better.

Take in another super big breath and then blow out all of the air.

5. Positive Taps
Tap down the points as you say the following:

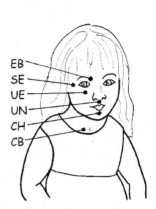

> EB: I am letting the anger go.
> SE: I can let it go now and forever.
> UE: I do not feel angry anymore.
> UN: I feel happy and peaceful.
> CH: I am making good choices.
> CB: I am free of this anger.

6. Rate the Intensity
Select on a scale of 0 to 10 how much anger you feel, with 10 being the most intense and 0 being not at all.

0	1	2	3	4	5	6	7	8	9	10

Homework
Repeat this process every time you feel angry or mad.

Anxious/Anxiety

1. Rate the Intensity

Select on a scale of 0 to 10 how much anxiety you feel, with 10 being the most intense and 0 being not at all.

0	1	2	3	4	5	6	7	8	9	10

2. Set up

Keep tapping the karate chop point the whole time as you say the following:

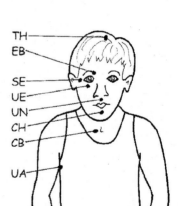

> Even though I feel anxious, I am awesome.
> Even though I feel so anxious, I am a good person.
> Even though I feel very anxious, I will allow this feeling to go away.

3. Negative Taps

Tap down the points as you say the following:

> EB: I feel anxious.
> SE: I feel nervous.
> UE: I am worried and upset.
> UN: I feel helpless.
> CH: I cannot handle this.
> CB: I cannot get through it.
> UA: I feel so anxious.
> TH: All of the left over anxiety.

Stop tapping.

Take in a super big breath and then blow out all of the air.

4. Forgiving
Hold your hand over your heart as you say the following:

I forgive myself for feeling anxious; I am doing my best.

Take in another super big breath and then blow out all of the air.

5. Positive Taps
Tap down the points as you say the following:

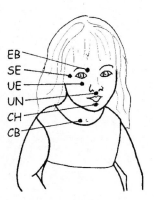

EB: I am letting go of the anxiety.
SE: I can let it go now and forever.
UE: I am free from this feeling.
UN: I feel calm. I am tapping into joy.
CH: I am not anxious anymore.
CB: I am safe and calm. I am protected.

6. Rate the Intensity
Select on a scale of 0 to 10 how much anxiety you feel, with 10 being the most intense and 0 being not at all.

0	1	2	3	4	5	6	7	8	9	10

Homework
Repeat this process every time you feel anxious. You can even do this process any time you think you will become anxious about something.

Frustrated

1. Rate the Intensity
Select on a scale of 0 to 10 how frustrated you feel, with 10 being the most intense and 0 being not at all.

0	1	2	3	4	5	6	7	8	9	10

2. Set up
Keep tapping the karate chop point the whole time as you say the following:

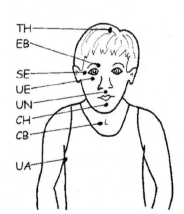

> Even though I am frustrated,
> I deeply and completely accept myself.
> Even though I feel very frustrated, I am a good person.
> Even though I am really frustrated, I know I will be able to let it go.

3. Negative Taps
Tap down the points as you say the following:

> EB: It is so frustrating.
> SE: I cannot take it anymore.
> UE: I do not feel I have any control.
> UN: I cannot feel peaceful and calm.
> CH: I am angry and frustrated.
> CB: This feels really bad.
> UA: It really aggravates me and makes me mad.
> TH: All of the left over feelings of being frustrated.

Stop tapping.
Take in a super big breath and then blow out all of the air.

4. Forgiving

Hold your hand over your heart as you say the following:

> I forgive myself for getting frustrated; I am doing the best I can.
> I forgive anything and anybody that frustrated me because I know they are doing their best too!

Take in another super big breath and then blow out all of the air.

5. Positive Taps

Tap down the points as you say the following:

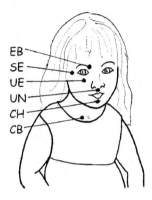

> EB: I am patient.
> SE: I can let go of the frustration.
> UE: I feel calm.
> UN: I feel peaceful. I am tapping into joy.
> CH: I feel in control.
> CB: I am not angry at myself anymore.

6. Rate the Intensity

Select on a scale of 0 to 10 how frustrated you feel, with 10 being the most intense and 0 being not at all.

0	1	2	3	4	5	6	7	8	9	10

Homework

Repeat this process two or three times per day when you are feeling frustrated.

Getting Yelled At

1. Rate the Intensity

Select on a scale of 0 to 10 how much getting yelled at bothers you, with 10 being the most intense and 0 being not at all.

0	1	2	3	4	5	6	7	8	9	10

2. Set up

Keep tapping the karate chop point the whole time as you say the following:

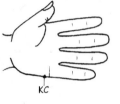

> Even though I got yelled at, I am a really good person.
> Even though I think I always get yelled at, I know I am awesome.
> Even though I feel scared and ashamed when I get yelled at, I know I can make good choices and follow the rules.

3. Negative Taps

Tap down the points as you say the following:

> EB: I got yelled at.
> SE: I feel embarrassed.
> UE: I feel shame.
> UN: I feel sad.
> CH: I've let someone down.
> CB: I must be wrong. They must not love me anymore.
> UA: It hurts my feelings.
> TH: All of the left over bad feelings about getting yelled at.

Stop tapping.

Take in a super big breath and then blow out all of the air.

4. Forgiving
Hold your hand over your heart as you say the following:

I forgive myself for getting yelled at; I am doing my best.
I forgive whoever yelled at me; they are doing their best too.

Take in another super big breath and then blow out all of the air.

5. Positive Taps
Tap down the points as you say the following:

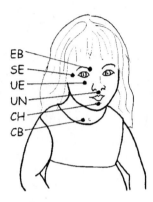

EB: I am letting the fear go.
SE: I am not afraid of getting yelled at.
UE: I am perfect the way I am.
UN: I learn from my mistakes.
CH: I do forgive myself.
CB: I am OK.

6. Rate the Intensity
Select on a scale of 0 to 10 how much getting yelled at bothers you, with 10 being the most intense and 0 being not at all.

0	1	2	3	4	5	6	7	8	9	10

Homework
Repeat this process a few times every day until you are sure you feel better about the situation.

Grief – Loss of Loved One

1. Rate the Intensity
Select on a scale of 0 to 10 how much grief you feel, with 10 being the most intense and 0 being not at all.

0	1	2	3	4	5	6	7	8	9	10

2. Set up
Keep tapping the karate chop point the whole time as you say the following:

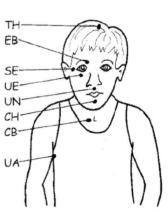

Please fill in the name of the person in the blanks.

> Even though I am sad that _____ died, I am safe.
> Even though I am mad that _____ had to die, I know they loved me.
> Even though I am really, really sad, I am getting better every day.

3. Negative Taps
Tap down the points as you say the following:

> EB: I am so sad.
> SE: Why did _____ have to go away?
> UE: I miss _____ so much.
> UN: I am angry that _____ died.
> CH: I am afraid that someone else will die too. I am scared.
> CB: What will happen to me now?
> UA: I have so many questions and so much sadness.
> TH: All of the left over sadness.

Stop tapping.
Take in a super big breath and then blow out all of the air.

4. Forgiving

Hold your hand over your heart as you say the following:

I forgive myself for being sad; it is really hard, but I am doing my best.

I forgive _____ for dying; they didn't mean to make me sad.

Take in another super big breath and then blow out all of the air.

5. Positive Taps

Tap down the points as you say the following:

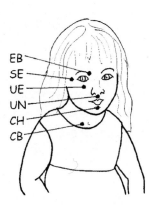

EB: I am feeling better.

SE: I can let go of the sadness.

UE: It is OK that I miss _____.

UN: I can remember the happy times with _____.

CH: Letting go of the sad, empty feeling.

CB: Feeling grateful and happy that I knew _____ and shared his/her life.

6. Rate the Intensity

Select on a scale of 0 to 10 how much grief you feel, with 10 being the most intense and 0 being not at all.

0	1	2	3	4	5	6	7	8	9	10

Homework

Repeat this process every day or whenever you feel sad about your loss. There are often secondary issues that will surface after the grief is resolved. Consider working on other segments, such as, "Fear", "Guilt", or "Anger".

Note to parents: Please see a qualified practitioner if your child is unable to resolve their grief.

Grief – Loss of Pet

1. Rate the Intensity
Select on a scale of 0 to 10 how much grief you feel, with 10 being the most intense and 0 being not at all.

0	1	2	3	4	5	6	7	8	9	10

2. Set up
Keep tapping the karate chop point the whole time as you say the following:

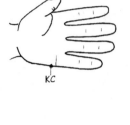

> Even though my pet died,
> I will be OK.
> Even though I miss _____, I am perfect how I am.
> Even though I am sad, it is not my fault.

3. Negative Taps
Tap down the points as you say the following:

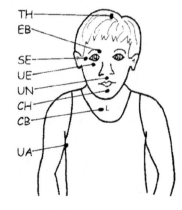

> EB: I am so sad.
> SE: I miss _____.
> UE: I could have done something to save _____. I blame myself.
> UN: I cannot stop thinking about it.
> CH: I cannot go on. My heart feels empty inside.
> CB: Nobody knows how I feel. Why did this happen?
> UA: How could _____ leave me? It is not fair.
> TH: All of the left over sadness and grief.

Stop tapping.
Take in a super big breath and then blow out all of the air.

4. Forgiving
Hold your hand over your heart as you say the following:

I forgive myself for being sad; I am doing the best I know how.

I forgive _____ for dying; he/she was my faithful friend and doesn't want me to be sad.

Take in another super big breath and then blow out all of the air.

5. Positive Taps
Tap down the points as you say the following:

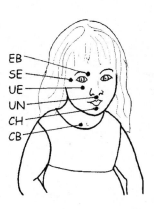

EB: I am able to let go of the sadness.

SE: I can let it go.

UE: I am free of this sadness.

UN: I am free from the grief.

CH: I am enjoying the good memories. I am tapping in the joy.

CB: I am happy at last.

6. Rate the Intensity
Select on a scale of 0 to 10 how much grief you feel, with 10 being the most intense and 0 being not at all.

0	1	2	3	4	5	6	7	8	9	10

Homework
Repeat this process until you feel better.

Note to parents: Please see a qualified energy therapist or EFT practitioner if your child is having a particularly difficult time resolving their grief. They deserve to be free from this grief.

Guilt

1. Rate the Intensity
Select on a scale of 0 to 10 how much this guilt bothers you, with 10 being the most intense and 0 being not at all.

0	1	2	3	4	5	6	7	8	9	10

2. Set up
Keep tapping the karate chop point the whole time as you say the following:

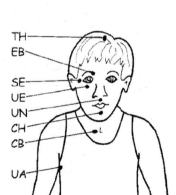

KC

> Even though I feel guilty, I didn't mean any harm.
> Even though I did something wrong, I am a good person.
> Even though I feel guilty, I am perfect just the way I am.

3. Negative Taps
Tap down the points as you say the following:

> EB: I feel guilt.
> SE: I feel ashamed. I feel embarrassed.
> UE: I feel remorse. I am feeling sorry for what I did or said.
> UN: I feel sadness.
> CH: It feels really bad.
> CB: I can never forgive myself.
> UA: I am feeling guilty.
> TH: Any and all of the left over guilt.

Stop tapping.
Take in a super big breath and then blow out all of the air.

4. Forgiving

Hold your hand over your heart as you say the following:

I forgive myself for what I did or said; I am doing my best.

I forgive myself for feeling guilty; I am the best person I can be.

Take in another super big breath and then blow out all of the air.

5. Positive Taps

Tap down the points as you say the following:

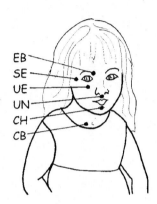

EB: I am letting go of the guilt.

SE: I can let it go.

UE: I won't do it again.

UN: I've learned a valuable lesson.

CH: I am free from this guilt.

CB: I am proud of myself.

6. Rate the Intensity

Select on a scale of 0 to 10 how much this guilt bothers you, with 10 being the most intense and 0 being not at all.

0	1	2	3	4	5	6	7	8	9	10

Homework

Repeat the process until the guilt is gone and you feel empowered to make good choices.

Hard to Pay Attention

1. Rate the Intensity
Select on a scale of 0 to 10 how hard it is for you to pay attention, with 10 being the most intense and 0 being not at all.

0	1	2	3	4	5	6	7	8	9	10

2. Set up
Keep tapping the karate chop point the whole time as you say the following:

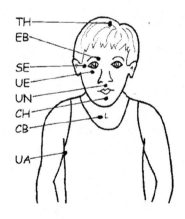

> Even though it is really hard to pay attention, I am perfect the way I am.
> Even though I cannot pay attention, I am an awesome kid!
> Even though it is frustrating when I cannot concentrate, I am a smart person.

3. Negative Taps
Tap down the points as you say the following:

> EB: I cannot pay attention.
> SE: I am not interested in this. It is boring.
> UE: I cannot focus.
> UN: My mind wanders.
> CH: I want to think of other things.
> CB: I do not care about this.
> UA: I cannot learn this. If I learn it, I will be expected to remember it.
> TH: All of the left over problems with paying attention.

Stop tapping.
Take in a super big breath and then blow out all of the air.

4. Forgiving
Hold your hand over your heart as you say the following:

I forgive myself for not being able to concentrate; I am doing my best.
I forgive everything for being so difficult.

Take in another super big breath and then blow out all of the air.

5. Positive Taps
Tap down the points as you say the following:

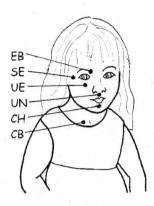

EB: I am letting go of anything that blocks my attention.
SE: I can let it all go.
UE: It is safe for me to pay attention.
UN: I can focus.
CH: It is getting easier all the time.
CB: Everything is becoming clear.

6. Rate the Intensity
Select on a scale of 0 to 10 how hard it is for you to pay attention, with 10 being the most intense and 0 being not at all.

0	1	2	3	4	5	6	7	8	9	10

Homework
Notice any trouble you are having with paying attention. Repeat this process as often as you feel you need to. You may also wish to work on the "Frustrated" segment of this book.

Diet and toxins play a significant role in a child's ability to focus and pay attention. Consider sensitivity screening to determine if certain foods or environmental conditions are a factor in your child's inability to pay attention.

Impatient

1. Rate the Intensity

Select on a scale of 0 to 10 how impatient you feel, with 10 being the most intense and 0 being not at all.

0	1	2	3	4	5	6	7	8	9	10

2. Set up

Keep tapping the karate chop point the whole time as you say the following:

KC

> Even though I am feeling impatient,
> I am a good person.
> Even though I cannot wait patiently, I am an awesome kid.
> Even though I cannot stand waiting any longer, I am a good person.

3. Negative Taps

Tap down the points as you say the following:

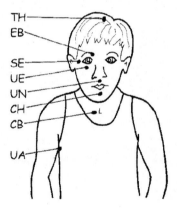

> EB: I cannot wait.
> SE: I feel restless.
> UE: I cannot wait another minute.
> UN: I won't be happy until _____.
> CH: I cannot possibly be happy unless _____.
> CB: Feeling impatient.
> UA: I'll never be able to wait for this.
> TH: All of the left over feeling like I cannot wait.

Stop tapping.

Take in a super big breath and then blow out all of the air.

4. Forgiving

Hold your hand over your heart as you say the following:

I forgive myself for being impatient; I am doing my best.

I forgive myself for being restless; I have done the best I know how.

Take in another super big breath and then blow out all of the air.

5. Positive Taps

Tap down the points as you say the following:

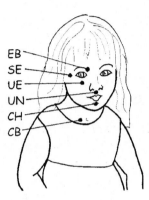

EB: I am letting go of the restlessness.

SE: I can be free of this problem.

UE: I am patient.

UN: I can wait.

CH: I am tapping into joy.

CB: I am calm and peaceful.

6. Rate the Intensity

Select on a scale of 0 to 10 how impatient you feel, with 10 being the most intense and 0 being not at all.

| 0 | 1 | 2 | 3 | 4 | 5 | 6 | 7 | 8 | 9 | 10 |

Homework

Repeat this process two or more times per day until you are no longer feeling impatient. You can think about what it is you are feeling impatient about while you are tapping.

Lost Something Special

1. Rate the Intensity
Select on a scale of 0 to 10 how much it bothers you that you lost something special, with 10 being the most intense and 0 being not at all.

0	1	2	3	4	5	6	7	8	9	10

2. Set up
Keep tapping the karate chop point the whole time as you say the following:

KC

> Even though I lost _____, I am a good kid.
> Even though I am sad about losing it, I am an awesome kid.
> Even though I do not know what I will do without it, I am OK.

3. Negative Taps
Tap down the points as you say the following:

> EB: I am sad.
> SE: I will never see it again.
> UE: I lost it for good.
> UN: I didn't mean to lose it.
> CH: I will never find it.
> CB: It can never be replaced.
> UA: I feel bad about not being responsible.
> TH: All of the left over sad feelings about losing something special.

TH
EB
SE
UE
UN
CH
CB
UA

Stop tapping.
Take in a super big breath and then blow out all of the air.

4. Forgiving

Hold your hand over your heart as you say the following:

I forgive myself for losing it; I am doing my best.

I forgive myself for feeling sad; I am doing the best I can.

Take in another super big breath and then blow out all of the air.

5. Positive Taps

Tap down the points as you say the following:

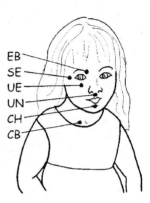

EB: I am letting go of the sadness.

SE: I am letting it go.

UE: I am free from this sadness.

UN: I just may find it one day.

CH: For now, I can let go of being mad at myself.

CB: I have learned to be more responsible.

6. Rate the Intensity

Select on a scale of 0 to 10 how much it bothers you that you lost this special thing, with 10 being the most intense and 0 being not at all.

0	1	2	3	4	5	6	7	8	9	10

Homework
Repeat this process every day until you feel better!

Loud Noises

1. Rate the Intensity
Select on a scale of 0 to 10 how much loud noises bother you, with 10 being the most intense and 0 being not at all.

0	1	2	3	4	5	6	7	8	9	10

2. Set up
Keep tapping the karate chop point the whole time as you say the following:

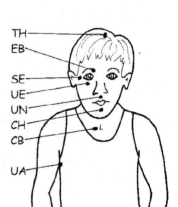

KC

> Even though I do not like loud noises,
> I am an awesome kid.
> Even though I am afraid of loud noises, I am OK with who I am.
> Even though I remember a time when loud noises or loud voices scared me, I am OK now.

3. Negative Taps
Tap down the points as you say the following:

> EB: Loud noises scare me.
> SE: Loud noises remind me of something bad.
> UE: It is loud.
> UN: I do not like it.
> CH: It is so loud. It feels like chaos.
> CB: It is scary. I have to get away from the loudness.
> UA: Loud noises mean trouble.
> TH: All of the left over problems with loud noises.

Stop tapping.

Take in a super big breath and then blow out all of the air.

4. Forgiving

Hold your hand over your heart as you say the following:

I forgive myself for not liking loud noises; I am doing my best.
I forgive loud noises and people with loud voices; they are doing their best too.

Take in another super big breath and then blow out all of the air.

5. Positive Taps

Tap down the points as you say the following:

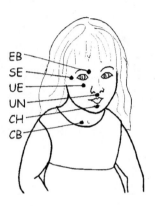

EB: I am letting go of the problems with loud noises.
SE: I can let it go now and forever.
UE: I am safe.
UN: I do not have to be bothered by the loud noises anymore.
CH: I am free from this problem.
CB: I am no longer uncomfortable with loud noises.

6. Rate the Intensity

Select on a scale of 0 to 10 how much the thought of loud noises bothers you, with 10 being the most intense and 0 being not at all.

0	1	2	3	4	5	6	7	8	9	10

Homework

Close your eyes and imagine being in a situation that has bothered you in the past because of the loudness. See how it makes you feel now. If thinking about the loudness bothers you, continue to repeat this process daily until you feel comfortable with that memory. This should help you tolerate loudness better.

Sadness

1. Rate the Intensity
Select on a scale of 0 to 10 how much sadness you feel, with 10 being the most intense and 0 being not at all.

0	1	2	3	4	5	6	7	8	9	10

2. Set up
Keep tapping the karate chop point the whole time as you say the following:

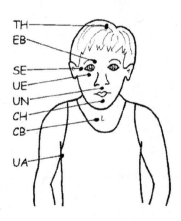

> Even though I feel sad, I am an awesome person.
> Even though I am sad, I love and accept myself.
> Even though I feel very sad, I can let the sadness go away and be happy.

3. Negative Taps
Tap down the points as you say the following:

> EB: I am sad.
> SE: I feel very sad.
> UE: It feels so bad.
> UN: I'll never feel happy again.
> CH: I can never let go of this sadness.
> CB: I just cannot do it. It is too hard.
> UA: I am too sad to smile.
> TH: All of the left over sadness.

Stop tapping.

Take in a super big breath and then blow out all of the air.

4. Forgiving
Hold your hand over your heart as you say the following:
> I forgive myself for being sad; I am doing the best that I know how.

Take in another super big breath and then blow out all of the air.

5. Positive Taps
Tap down the points as you say the following:

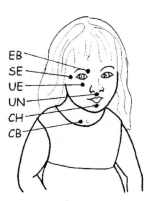

EB: I am letting go of the sad feelings.
SE: I can be free from feeling sad.
UE: I am happy. I am tapping into joy.
UN: I can be happy every day.
CH: I can smile again and feel really good about it.
CB: I am happy and free.

6. Rate the Intensity
Select on a scale of 0 to 10 how much sadness you feel, with 10 being the most intense and 0 being not at all.

0	1	2	3	4	5	6	7	8	9	10

Homework
Repeat this process two to three times per day for two weeks and anytime you feel sad.

Note to parents: If your child suffers from deep sadness, please consider taking them to an EFT practitioner or qualified therapist. You child deserves to live their life in joy.

Trouble Sleeping

1. Rate the Intensity
Select on a scale of 0 to 10 how much sleeping bothers you, with 10 being the most intense and 0 being not at all.

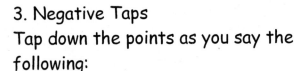

0	1	2	3	4	5	6	7	8	9	10

2. Set up
Keep tapping the karate chop point the whole time as you say the following:

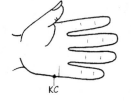

KC

    Even though I am afraid to go to sleep,
    I can feel safe in my bed.
    Even though it is hard to fall asleep, I rock!
    Even though I cannot sleep, I am an awesome kid.

3. Negative Taps
Tap down the points as you say the following:

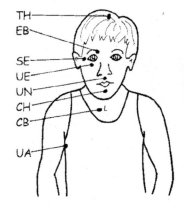

    EB: It is hard to fall asleep.
    SE: There are so many things to think about.
    UE: It is easy to look around.
    UN: I do not want to sleep. It is not safe to sleep.
    CH: I want to stay up.
    CB: I might miss something if I fall asleep.
    UA: If something happens, I won't know it.
    TH: All of the left over fear of sleeping.

Stop tapping.
Take in a super big breath and then blow out all of the air.

4. Forgiving
Hold your hand over your heart as you say the following:

I forgive myself for not wanting to sleep; I am doing my best.
I forgive sleep for sometimes being hard; it is getting easier.

Take in another super big breath and then blow out all of the air.

5. Positive Taps
Tap down the points as you say the following:

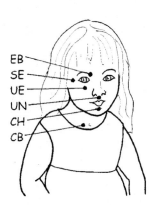

EB: I am safe when I sleep.
SE: I can let myself fall asleep.
UE: Sleep is good for me.
UN: Sleep helps me to be healthy.
CH: Sleep helps me to get strong.
CB: I have nothing to fear.

6. Rate the Intensity
Select on a scale of 0 to 10 how hard it is for you to sleep, with 10 being the most intense and 0 being not at all.

0	1	2	3	4	5	6	7	8	9	10

Homework
When you go to bed tonight, let your whole body relax, and make yourself feel safe and cozy. Close your eyes and imagine you are lying on a soft fluffy cloud.

Note to parents: You may also want to have your child work on the "Fear of the Dark," "Fear of Monsters," "I Cannot Do It," "Staying in Bed," or "Fear of Enclosed Places" segments of this book.

RESOURCES

Contact Information for the author:

E-mail: info@tapintobalance.com

Web sites: www.tapintobalance.com
www.tapintojoy.net

To schedule in person or telephone sessions with Susan, to send testimonials of how this book has helped you and your child, to order additional copies of this book, to order Gary Craig's EFT training videos, to link to the eft4kids forum, or for links to other wonderful Web sites, please visit:
 www.tapintobalance.com

ABOUT THE AUTHOR

Susan is an Energy Therapist. She currently sees people and animals of all ages in her private practice. She uses a variety of therapies including EFT, EAV (electro-acupuncture according to Voll), herbs, homeopathy, and nutritional counseling to restore energetic balance to the body.

Susan is a graduate of St. Mary's University of Minnesota and is a Certified Natural Health Professional. She is a student and an educator. Before getting involved in energy therapies, she spent years working as an Environmental Biologist and as a corporate Research Scientist. She has several peer-reviewed papers in scientific journals to her credit. Susan is an advocate of health freedom and environmental awareness. She has told her story in a television interview and on her Web site.

Susan lives in Palos Heights, Illinois with her husband Scott and their three amazing sons.